Duquesne Studies

LANGUAGE AND LITERATURE SERIES

[VOLUME TWELVE]

GENERAL EDITOR:

Albert C. Labriola, *Department of English, Duquesne University*

ADVISORY EDITOR:

Foster Provost, *Department of English, Duquesne University*

EDITORIAL BOARD:

Judith H. Anderson
Donald Cheney
Patrick Cullen
French R. Fogle
A.C. Hamilton
S.K. Heninger, Jr.
A. Kent Hieatt
Robert B. Hinman
William B. Hunter
Michael Lieb
Waldo F. McNeir
Thomas P. Roche, Jr.
John T. Shawcross
James D. Simmonds
John M. Steadman
Humphrey Tonkin
Robert F. Whitman

John Milton and Influence

John Milton and Influence

Presence in Literature, History and Culture

John T. Shawcross

Duquesne University Press
Pittsburgh, Pennsylvania

Published in the United States of America
by Duquesne University Press
600 Forbes Avenue
Pittsburgh, Pennsylvania 15282-0101

Library of Congress Cataloging-in-Publication Data

Shawcross, John T.
  John Milton and influence : presence in literature, history, and
culture / John T. Shawcross.
     p.   cm. — (Duquesne studies. Language and literature series
; v. 12)
  Includes bibliographical references and index.
  ISBN 0–8207–0235–8 : $27.95
  1. Milton, John, 1608–1674—Influence.   2. Literature,
Modern—18th century—History and criticism.   3. Influence
(Literary, artistic, etc.)   4. Civilization, Modern—18th century.
I. Title.   II. Series.
PR3588.S467   1991
809'.033—dc20   91–18635
                                                                      CIP

Contents

Introduction
by Way of Preface

The ten essays that now make up the chapters of this volume were written over the last few years, most for oral presentation at various literary conferences, but none has been previously published. They all look at the question of influence, some through direct influence, some through indirect. Their concern is not, however, that of source-hunting with little interest beyond demonstration of source. Indeed, the first essay on Shakespeare and Milton is specifically opposed to that kind of outdated statement of alleged debt, and for the most part finds it wanting. Scholars of the past often sought sources only, though their results have manifested their knowledge of these two authors and their ignorance of others. But deep influence is more elusive than that, lying in the tone and fabric of the later works, in a rhythm or a nuance of meaning. When the influence shows itself overtly, it may be—or at least for the knowledgeable reader it becomes—an allusion, placed there by the author to ask the reader to recall the earlier reference as context and commentary, not simply as word or image recognition.

Milton's allusion in "Upon the Circumcision" to Philippians 2.6–8, depicting the kenosis of Christ, when he wrote, "for us frail dust/Emptied his glory, ev'n to nakednes" (11. 19–20), is directing the reader to understand that we must humble ourselves in order to be exalted as the epistle continues to speak of the Son. It is not only that the Son took on the likeness of humans, but that humankind itself should emulate him in humility. Milton proceeds in the poem, "And that great Cov'nant which we still transgress/Intirely satisfi'd," implying that humankind has not satisfied the covenant despite the frequent outward appearance of having done so. We have not emptied ourselves of whatever is our human glory: We have not become humble, and thus cannot look forward to exaltation at the end of time. "That great Cov'nant" is clearly not "the Covenant of Works, embodied in the Mosaic law" as A. S. P. Woodhouse and Douglas Bush unusefully say in a *A Variorum Commentary on the Poems of John Milton.*[1] It is the covenant made with Abraham (Genesis 17.7, 10), implying obedience to God's will: "And I will establish my covenant between me and thee and thy seed after thee in their generations, for an everlasting covenant, to be God unto thee and to thy seed after thee" ; "This is my covenant, which ye shall keep, between me and you and thy seed after thee; Every man child among you shall be circumcised." Of course, this second allusion is particularly apt in a poem "Upon the Circumcision" of Jesus. But though there are those who offer outward show of the covenant by circumcision, they still transgress it by not "seal[ing] obedience."

The allusion encompassed by the " source" of the last two lines of "L'Allegro" ("These delights, if thou canst give, /Mirth with thee I mean to live," 151–52) and "Il

Penseroso" ("These pleasures *Melancholy* give, /And I with thee will choose to live," 175–76) is to Christopher Marlowe's "The Passionate Shepherd to His Love" : "If these delights thy mind may move, /Then live with me, and be my love." The allusion should have led to two realizations about Milton's companion poems, which also are notably influenced by lines from John Fletcher and from Robert Burton: first, Milton wishes his reader to contrast his moral, action-filled, self-satisfying, cerebral pleasures with Marlowe's sensuous and tangible lures; and second, readers should see in the poems the writer writing a variation upon a theme). In the context of the allusion, Milton's companion poems much less represent his "ideal" activities and two sides to his personality than critics have conjured up.

Milton's influence upon succeeding poets and thinkers falls into various areas: the poetic in form and versification, in subject matter and treatment within the poem, in concepts involved in political and governmental theory, or aesthetics, or landscape, or gender relations and societal concerns. As with any influential writer, Milton may supply a reference of surface importance only, or one of deep-seated control over another's thought or writing, and there may be allusive influence as well; as in the examples above, the reader is expected to insert the context of the original into the context of a present text. This is the intertextuality that has become a critical byword in recent years. The essays here set forth the pervasiveness of Milton's influence among ordinary people, gifted and not very gifted writers, theoreticians and practical doers. Most of the authors and works discussed date from the eighteenth century, with some spill over into the nineteenth, and poetry, the novel, and belles lettres are cited. The upshot of these essays is the importance in studying Milton as source and inspiration and presence, and avoiding such study can flirt with superficial reading and understanding. While an anxiety of influence may hang over some of these writers and works—William Mason, "Vallombrosa"—the Milton that this influence delineates is an admired force to be enveloped or to be ever like a star apart, an observation better stating Wordsworth's position and others' following after the seventeenth century giant than Milton's position within his own world.

Yet another aspect of influence should reverse our reading direction. Do we not know William Butler Yeats by comprehending W. H. Auden's perceptions? or Robert Browning by viewing Ezra Pound's dramatic monologues and Canto II? And may we not come to read Milton "better" by seeing what Alexander Pope does with the opening of the second book of *Paradise Lost* in his *Dunciad*? or recognize strikingly what negative possibilities lie in the creation of humankind by a God who can become an "incensed Deitie," exclaiming, "ingrate," when we observe The Monster loosed to himself by a Frankenstein? (I wonder how many readers, though, experience the point of Mary Shelley's calling her novel by the name of the creative force, not The Monster or Man.) The final essay explores this "reversed" influence by using James Joyce's employment of Milton's poems to read Milton's poems in a somewhat different light. This reading recognizes the evidence of the artistic talent of Joyce, leading us to understand what Joyce saw as Milton's " message" or at least to provide corroboration of what we might have sensed.

ONE

Shakespeare, Milton and Literary Debt

F requent over the centuries have been discussions of John Milton's debt to William Shakespeare. When analyzed, however, the alleged parallels generally disappear into the common stock of poetic language and tradition, or dissolve as unrelated items brought together by a zealous critic. I shall be trying to rid Milton of certain limitations of the critics in order to suggest a literary debt by way of allusion, subtle remembrance, and unconscious echo, inadequately appreciated if only the kind of alleged verbal echoes offered up so profusely in the past is evidence of that debt. Recently some of these parallels have been labeled "transumption" or "metalepsis."

There are two basic ways to approach literary debts: one external through allusions and demonstrable knowledge of one author by another, and one internal through verbal, contextual, or structural reminiscences, if not downright quotation or adaptation. Perhaps, too, a case can be made from negative evidence, when one author's knowledge of the other is certain, suggesting a conscious effort to disguise influence. In the case of Shakespeare and Milton we have two of the most important British authors, well known and well read by various students of literature, and thus the critical conclusion that the later, Milton, knew and echoed the former, Shakespeare. One of the problems, however, is that some of the proffered evidence—indeed most of the verbal evidence—does not support that. It tells us, instead, that the commentator knew Shakespeare's and Milton's works very well, but apparently knew little about other authors and various literary traditions. The eighteenth century editors of both authors often postulated that kind of literary debt, and nineteenth and twentieth century commentators have often simply followed along. For example, Alwin Thaler in a paper first published in *PMLA* in 1925 and revised for *Shakspere's Silences* (1929) writes: "This universal frame, this wondrous fair' (*P.L.* 5.154–155). Undoubtedly both Shakspere and Milton drew upon the eighth Psalm, but Milton is nonetheless indebted to Shakspere."[1] Henry John Todd, in editing Milton, also paralleled Shakespeare's line from *Hamlet* 2.2.309, with *PL* 8.15.[2] Of course, there are numerous other analogues to the line and to the idea, probably all ultimately drawn from the eighth psalm, such as Joshua Sylvester's rendition of Du Bartas, the First and Seventh Days giving examples; John Wilkins's *Discourse Concerning A New Planet* 2.6 and 2.9; and Sir John Davies, *Orchestra*, stanzas 33–34.

Many of the parallels of Shakespeare and Milton cited are presented as illustrations of language and as explanation of an idea rather than to infer literary debt, yet some, like Thaler, made such inferences from those same illustrations. The belief that Milton is greater because of this "debt" to Shakespeare seems prevalent; that Milton is somehow lesser because of such "debt" is also conspicuous. We might note William Warburton's comment concerning "Comus": "Milton has here more professedly imitated the manner of Shakespeare in his fairy scenes, than in any other of his works: and his poem is much the better for it, not only for the beauty, variety, and novelty of his images, but for a brighter vein of poetry, and an ease and delicacy of expression very superior to his natural manner."[3]

It is impossible to prove that one author did not use or remember another, almost always, but should there be numerous other possible sources for a parallel, the debt of one to the other may be suspect. For example, the con- junction of justice and mercy can be found in most of the writings of the Elizabethan, deriving from the traditions of Psalm 85 (which Milton translated, incidentally) and its rendition as the Parliament in Heaven (and see *Piers Plowman* as well). Yet Todd paralleled PL 10.58–60, 77–78, with *Merchant of Venice* 4.1.196–97, and Thaler, with *Measure for Measure* 2.2.75–78. Among analogues that Milton might have known are lines from *The Tragedie of Claudius Tiberius Nero* and Giles Fletcher's *Christ's Victorie in Heaven;* and George Wither's *The History of the Pestilence*, then unprinted, employed the conjunction twice.

This attitude led Ethel Seaton, in an essay on Shakes- peare's influence on "Comus," talking of the word *rind* in the masque (1.664) and *Romeo and Juliet* 2.3.23, to say, "An unexpected word which gives the reader of *Comus* pause can often be explained or justified by a parallel in the play."[4] Milton is talking of the body as "corporal rinde" and Shakespeare the "infant rind of this small flower." I doubt that most people are given pause by Milton's use of *rind* here; certainly not anyone who has read Spenser, who uses the word four times in a meaning more similar to Milton's (in *The Faerie Queene, The Shepheardes Calender, Ruines of Rome*, and *Daphnaida*). Or one can instance the curious paralleling of our two authors by Charles Dunster in a concatenation of verbal explanations. Sir Thomas Hanmer questioned Shakespeare's lines in *The Tempest* 4.1.66–67 ("thy broom groves,/ Whose shadow the dismissed bachelor loves"), and so changed the phrase to "brown groves."[5] Dunster then used that test to justify Milton's "alleys brown" in PR 2.293, but since "alleys" seemed so odd he added "pathes and alleies wide" from *FQ* 1.1.7.[6] Thomas P. Harrison explained Shakespeare's "broom groves,"[7] making any alleged parallel between Shakespeare and Milton in these lines to disappear.

Now we may say, quite rightly, that some of these parallels were not alleged as indicative of debts. Thomas Keightley, R.C. Browne, and David Masson in their editions of Milton's poetry all noted the induction, lines 1–16, to *2 Henry IV*, in connection with *Samson Agonistes* 970–74. And then Masson wrote: "The manner in which Fame is personified and equipped here seems due to Milton's own imagination. In Chaucer's *House of Fame* Fame is a goddess, attended by the wind-god Aeolus, with two trumpets—one a black trumpet of foul brass, which may be called the Infamy or Slander trumpet; the either a gold trumpet, or trumpet of Praise. In the 'contrary blast' Milton remembers this . . . ."[8] But Thaler, in his attempt to make Shakespeare Milton's source, states:

> Masson and other commentators have suggested that Milton's 'double-mouthed' Fame, as described in *Samson Agonistes*, is first cousin to Shakspere's Rumour, 'painted full of tongues.' And Rumour 'with a thousand tongues' speaks also in Milton's *Quintum Novembris*. Though Milton's Fame may owe something to Ovid, Virgil, and Chaucer, the family resemblance between it and Shakspere's loud-mouthed bearer of false or contradictory reports seems unmistakable. (179)

One will find the "double-mouth'd" Fame also in Marlowe's *Epigrame*, "In Afrum. 40," in George Chapman's *Hero and Leander*, and in three of Robert Herrick's poems.

(I cite only a few examples here of these frequent analogues, all of which Milton could have easily come by.)

But the debt inferred has not been only in words and phrases but in ideas, characterizations, situations, scenes, and metrics. The single, full published study of such a relationship between Milton and Shakespeare is Alwin Thaler's, already cited. Thaler concluded: 1) "Shakesperian memories . . . took deep impression upon the heart of his [Milton's] poetic fancy in youth, sustained and enriched his epic flights with an infinite variety of dramatic motifs and devices, and helped to establish in the unequalled masterpieces of his declining years a remarkable balance between Greek and Elizabethan dramatic forms"; 2) "Out of approximately 250 reminiscent passages in Milton here examined, about 75 are from *Comus* and early poems; about 165 or 170 from *Paradise Lost, Paradise Regained,* and *Samson Agonistes* (some 120, 20, and 30 respectively); and some 10 from the prose pamphlets"; 3) of the 35 plays considered, only *Much Ado* and *Comedy of Errors* are not in some way represented, and "If from this list we subtract the eight or ten plays which seem not to have yielded at least two or more fairly certain echoes, there remain 25 which Milton did not forget, and these include the greatest of the tragedies, histories, and comedies"; 4) "Two-thirds of Milton's Shaksperian recollection . . . [is] verbal or figurative"; and 5)

> In studying the evidence it is constantly to be remembered that the two poets drew upon a common stock of poetic diction and imagery, the heritage of the Renaissance. This fact, however, does not seriously diminish the sum total of Milton's verbal indebtedness to Shakspere. His borrowings vary in degree and kind. Some, especially his appropriations of descriptive nouns and adjectives, are as sharp and clean-cut as 'complete' steel, as sturdily obvious as clouted shoon treading upon his goodly frame, the earth. Others . . . draw in their train shadowy recollections of a

9

> turn of phrase, a cadence, or modulation well-loved though
> scarce remembered; and these have no less power to haunt
> and startle and waylay. Shakspere's personifications . . .
> are Milton's familiars as much as Shakspere's. Again,
> Shaksperian imagery is constantly recognizable in Milton's
> description of Nature—of flowers, birds, and trees, dawn
> and night, moon and stars and tempest, and in the visible
> forms he gives to such abstractions as sleep and war, death
> and peace. (see pp. 205–7 and n. 1)

The ten plays with only one echo referred to are *Titus Andronicus, The Merry Wives, Pericles, 1* and *3 Henry VI, The Two Gentlemen, Twelfth Night, The Taming of the Shrew, Timon,* and *Henry VIII. 2 Henry VI* and *The Winter's Tale* are retained "because one or two of the few echoes have been generally accepted as clear and unmistakable." The discarding of *Much Ado* was questioned by George Coffin Taylor.[9] *Hamlet* and *Macbeth* are found to be of first importance, then *Lear* and *Othello,* among the tragedies; *Richard II, 1* and *2 Henry IV,* and *Henry V,* with *Richard III* scarcely less important among the histories; *A Midsummer Night's Dream* and *The Tempest* among the comedies. According to this, Milton obviously agreed with later critics about which were the best plays! My own study has uncovered more than double the number of alleged parallels that Thaler listed—that is, 527— about 125 of which I dismiss as simply language illustration and definition.

The external approach to literary debt through allusion and demonstrable knowledge of one author by another is more interesting for what it says about the critics and critical climate than, in this case, about Shakespeare and Milton. The assumption of Milton's knowledge and admiration of Shakespeare (neither of which I deny and both of which I believe) brought Todd to attribute the passages on Shakespeare in Milton's nephew Edward Phillips's *Theatrum Poetarum* to Milton (Milton's alleged connection with the work was disproved some time ago by Sanford Golding[10]). David Masson in his *Life of John Milton* played with the idea that Milton, a child of six, may have seen Shakespeare on his last visit to London, 1614, had he walked boisterously down Bread Street after an uproarious time at the Mermaid, and Ernest Brennecke fancied that Milton, Senior may have met Shakespeare in 1601 through Thomas Morley, though there is no proof that Morley knew Milton, except that they both were musicians, or that Morley knew Shakespeare, except the song "It was a lover and his lass." Or, Brennecke also speculated, Milton may have known Shakespeare through George Peele, who acted with Shakespeare at Blackfriars and who collaborated with Milton. Should Shakespeare have need to have legal documents produced during his final London visit, the fantasy goes, he may have gone to John Milton, Scrivener, whom he may have previously met.

Francis Peck contended Miltonic authorship of the translation of George Buchanan's *Baptistes*, to show the other side of this coin of debt, because of the "seeming imitation(s) of Shakespeare, another practice very usual with Milton." (It might be pointed out that *Baptistes* will be found in some libraries separated from *New Memoirs of the Life and Writings of John Milton*, although it has continuous signatures and pagination, and catalogued as a work by Milton.) But the only known statement of Milton's knowledge or admiration of Shakespeare, aside from the works, is Bishop Thomas Newton's report that Elizabeth Minshull, Milton's widow, when "asked whom he approved most of our English poets . . . answered Spenser, Shakespeare, and Cowley."[11]

The first reference to Shakespeare in the Milton canon is "An Epitaph on the admirable Dramatic Poet, W. Shakespeare," prefixed to the Second Folio of Shakespeare's *Works*, 1632. It also appears in the 1640 edition of

Shakespeare's *Poems*, in the Third Folio, 1663–64, and in the Fourth Folio, 1685. There are three different forms of the text in these volumes, but Robert Metcalf Smith got them confused.[12] His Effigies C is the first text of 1632 (there are seven separate issues), *Poems*, the Third Folio (three issues) and the Fourth Folio (three issues). Effigies A and B occur in the pirated issues of 1640 or 1641; there is only one issue with A, two with B. Milton's encomium was printed in a different version in his poems in 1645, with the title "On Shakespear" and the date "1630," and reprinted in 1673. The occasion for its writing is unknown, although some conjectures have it that it was written expressly for an edition of Shakespeare, possibly that which materialized as the Second Folio. There was even the ludicrous idea at the beginning of the nineteenth century that Milton was the editor of the Second Folio. Today speculation has suggested that Milton's poem appeared in the volume through his acquaintance with Henry Lawes, the court musician, the most plausible explanation.[13]

The underlying question in the poem is that of the artist and world glory, an old theme, well presented by Spenser, Sidney, Daniel, Greville, Dyer, and Browne. Samuel Daniel in his *Epistle to the Lady Margaret, Countess of Cumberland* comes to the same conclusion as Milton here: the Lady Margaret has *Fame* because her goodness is *recorded in so many hearts*; thus it has *built a farre more exquisite and glorious dwelling then all the gold can frame.* Milton says that Shakespeare *in our wonder and astonishment* has *built* himself *a live-long Monument* because he has made *us Marble,* which is far greater than *piled Stones* or a *Star-ypointing Pyramid.*

A commonplace of critical opinion of Shakespeare in the seventeenth century was that he was a natural, born poet, one of "natures family," as Ben Jonson put it in his eulogy. The "slow-endeavouring art" is but Jonson's "second heat"; and there is no specific contrast that Milton is making between himself and Shakespeare. Milton was having trouble with *The Passion* at this time and had written little; he cannot have been audaciously comparing himself in the terms of "slow-endeavouring art" with the deservedly famed Shakespeare. With suspicious insistence, Jonson and others, including Milton, seem to contemplate the question of erecting a monument or the need for a monument. In all these poems the authors are attempting to achieve for Shakespeare some memorial. Jonson says that Shakespeare is a monument in himself; Leonard Digges that the works are the monument; Milton that the readers are. That idea, which has seemed exceptional to some people, is expressed in Browne's "On the Countess Dowager of Pembroke," his "Epitaph on His Wife," and his "Epitaph on William Hopton"; in Thomas Tomkys's *Albumazar* 1.4.3–4; in Massinger's *The Fatal Dowry* 2.1; in George Sandys's *Ovids Metamorphoses* 6.311–14; in *Caesar's Revenge* 1.1.120–22 and 3.2.1308–10; and in Davenant's *The Wits* 5.2.

The stock quality of Milton's epitaph may be pointed out by parts of many poems from Sidney's time to well after 1630; notable, however, is a partially similar verse at first attributed to Shakespeare, "An Epitaph on Sr Edward Standly. Ingraven on his Toombe in Tong Church":

> Not monumentall stones preserves our Fame;
> Nor sky-aspiring Piramides our name;
> The memory of him for whom this standes
> Shall outlive marble and defacers hands
>> When all to times consumption shall bee given,
>> Standly for whom this stands shall stand in Heaven.

Theodore Spencer listed as resemblances between the two poems: 1) the uselessness of the monument; 2) the rhyme of "Fame" and "name"; 3) the mention of marble; and 4) the term "sky-aspiring Piramides."[14] Although admitting that the first three are commonplace, Spencer believed that Milton followed this poem because he thought it was Shakespeare's. However, the language and idea of the fourth resemblance are evident in Horace, *Odes* 3.30.1–5; *Richard II* 1.3.129–30; *FQ* 5.10.23–24; *Ruines of Time*, 407–12 and also 421–27; Spenser's *Commendatory Sonnets* 3.1.8; *Caesar's Revenge* 1.6.597–99; and Browne's *Britannia's Pastorals* 2.1.1016–18.

Milton's "Epitaph" is an excellent original encomium that brings together many commonplaces in honor of a great poet. From the poem it may be inferred that Milton read Shakespeare and some of the praise of Shakespeare. How intensively or extensively Milton read Shakespeare, however, cannot be determined from the poem. There is nothing to indicate a greater knowledge or appreciation of Shakespeare than anyone else's knowledge or appreciation of him.

Yet the belief that Milton was well qualified to write critically of Shakespeare led Coleridge to interpret the ascription J. M. S. on the poem "A mind reflecting ages past" in the Second Folio as "John Milton, Student." A different view of Milton's attitude toward Shakespeare in this poem is the seed for John Guillory's analysis of Milton's anxiety over his predecessor. In *Poetic Authority: Spenser, Milton, and Literary History*, Guillory contends that Milton saw Shakespeare's achievement as the result of imaginative, irrational, secular poetry created *ex nihilo*, whereas his own, created *ex deo*, was sacred and revelatory. "The poem works toward its climax by opposing the fluid motion of Shakespeare's verse to the condition of stasis he induced in his hearers, and upon that abstract foundation Milton builds his conceit of the audience as monument."[15] Guillory, anxious over Harold Bloom and Leslie Brisman, sees Milton ultimately equating Shakespeare with Comus and hence with Satan.

Shakespeare's natural ability is reasserted in "L'Allegro," 133–34, and Peck, Newton, Edmond Malone, and John Bowles all believed Milton borrowed from the very person he was commending as "fancies child, Warbl[ing] his native Wood-notes wild." A. W. Verity asserted that those "woodnotes" were, specifically, *MND* and *Tempest* because "There are . . . more allusions in his poems to these two plays than to all the rest of Shakespeare's drama put together."[16] In his poem Milton is evoking images of mirth, lightheartedness, and happiness, and he thus moves to the comic stage, just previously having written of the fairy tradition, of dreams, of high romance, and then of Hymen in his saffron robe, "with Taper clear,/And pomp, and feast, and revelry,/With mask, and antique Pageantry." This leads him to think of the stage masques that have incorporated this tradition, and he writes of the most important dramatists of the age, of Jonson, who is "learned," and of Shakespeare, who is oppositely presented as natural, as in the "Epitaph." It is difficult to determine from this whether Milton did or did not have "a very keen sense of Shakespere's greatness." But certainly the reference and epithet are highly commendable.

Verity, unlike other critics, believed:

> The couplet in fact is faint praise, and it has been doubted whether Milton has a very keen sense of Shakespeare's greatness . . . The passages in which Milton can be held to have borrowed from Shakespeare's tragedies are very rare . . . It is therefore a tenable view that Milton's appreciation of Shakespeare is limited; probably it did not grow with his Puritanism. (91–92)

Verity, I suggest, depends on preconceived stereotypes.

The third and last allusion to Shakespeare in Milton's works occurs in a well-known (and much misread) passage in *Eikonoklastes*. Charles I, a known patron of the arts and the owner of numerous editions of Shakespeare's plays, according to Margaret Pickel,[17] was believed to have written *Eikon Basilike*, a most humble and reverential work. Accusing Charles of counterfeiting religious devotions as all tyrants have done, Milton quotes from Shakespeare's famous tyrant, Richard III, whom he likens in his expression of piety to Charles in his remarks. (Milton is attacking Charles, not Shakespeare, as Malone, who credited George Steevens, supposed.) This reference and quotation show that Milton read *Richard III* and that he remembered the historical role portrayed in the play of the hypocritically pious tyrant.

It may be concluded that Milton read Shakespeare with approbation; but how extensively or intensively he read Shakespeare and his patent opinion of him are not sharply defined.

There are some other Miltonic passages that have been taken to allude to Shakespeare or his works, and I note them so that no one feels compelled to resurrect them. Despite the remarks of Thomas Warton, A. W. Verity, W. Skeat, and Ida Langdon, lines 40–44 of "Elegia prima" refer to Greek and Senecan tragedy only: the *ferus ultor criminis* is not Banquo's ghost or the ghost in *Hamlet*; the *puer infelix* is not Romeo but Haemon in *Antigone*; and lines 37–46 talk of Pelops's progeny, Ilus's progeny, and the Oedipus plays. Likewise lines 101–02 of "Il Penseroso" have been taken to refer to Shakespeare by Bishop Richard Hurd and Thomas Keightley; Verity commented that "We may hope that this alludes to Shakespeare," and Martin Sampson iterated the thought.[18] However, the tragedy to which Milton is referring is again classical, and a similar preference for the classical is seen in the remarks on the dramatic poem prefacing *Samson Agonistes*.Shakespeare was probably in Milton's mind when he wrote of blank verse in "our best *English* Tragedies," but of course other Elizabethan dramatists fit, too. Skeat made the unique and absurd comment on lines 30–34 of "Mansus" that they are "Doubtless a reference to Shakespeare ('Sweet swan of Avon')." The swans are actual swans such as Spenser depicts on the Thames in "Prothalamion," which might have been in Milton's mind here and in lines 59–69.

Thaler referred the "Trinculo's" in *An Apology for Smectymnuus* to *The Tempest*—but the name had become commonplace because of Tomkys's *Albumazar*. Thaler also found Polonius to be "This Champion from behind the Arras," as had Frederick J. Furnivall, John Munro, and John A. St. John, before him.[19] The image is drawn from the stage and appears in Marston's *The Dutch Courtezan* 5.1.46–47, and John Day's *Law Tricks* III, as well as other Shakespearean plays. Milton's historical studies, when they verged upon historical characters and situations present in Shakespeare's drama, have been arrogated to Shakespearean sources as well. The remarks in *The History of Britain* on Cymbeline, Cassibelan, Macbeth, Edgar, Leir, and Cordeilla, the two lines in "Epitaphium Damonis," 164–65, mentioning Arviragus, and the Trinity Manuscript entries on Macbeth and Kenneth have all been confounded in some way with Shakespeare. Milton, when he calls some of Geoffrey's history untrue, is obviously not referring to Cymbeline's sons, as Thaler would have us believe; Milton's account of Leir and Cordeilla comes from Holinshed, as his spelling indicates as well. The story of Edgar is "fitter for a Novel then a History" because it sounds specious and romantic, not because Milton is the "literary artist in search of material." And surely there is no connection between Milton's Macbeth entry and Shakespeare's play, one of a number of subjects from Scotch history, even though

Peck, Steevens, John W. Hales, and Thaler were convinced there had to be.[20] And Thaler's curious allocation of Shakespeare as Milton's "late court poet" in 1660 in *The Ready and Easy Way* makes one wonder whether he knew the meanings of "late" and "court"; the reference is apparently to William Davenant.[21]

I seem to have set up straw men in citing these outrageously farfetched or indistinct examples, but they do define the criticism concerned with Milton's debt to Shakespeare and suggest the two points stated before: critics have known these two authors well, and since these are two of the greatest, there must be a debt of the later to the earlier.

The internal approach to literary debt, in the case of Shakespeare and Milton, is similarly harmed by over-zealous critics. As noted before, I have found 527 citations of Miltonic passages: *PL*, 222; "Comus," 94; *PR*, 48; *SA*, 46; Prose Works, 10; and others, 107. Numerous works are not included in this list: many of the prose works, many poems in foreign languages, many of the sonnets, almost all the translations, and "At a Solemn Music." Corresponding to these are 723 Shakespearean passages, some of which overlap or are repetitious and four of which are from works not in the present Shakespearean canon, but also some of which were cited for more than one Miltonic passage. These consist of all the plays and poems and many of the sonnets (there are 19 citations from the sonnets). The plays with the most citations are *MND*, 87; *Hamlet*, 63; *Romeo*, 60, *Tempest*, 52; *Macbeth*, 46; *Richard II*, 23; *Othello*, 22; *Antony* and *Caesar*, 21 each; and *1 Henry IV*, 20.

The sources of parallels are interesting. First, there is the use of a word that seems to strike the commentator as unusual. Another example from Seaton involves the word "jocund" in "Comus," 173 and 985, of which she wrote: These "may well be due to his classical reading; yet of the half-dozen or so times that the word is used by Shakespeare, none is so unforgettable as Romeo's" (3.5.9–10). Needless to say, we can find this word frequently. Thaler provides many examples of the paralleling of supposedly unusual words, like his printing of "Comus," 376–77 ("sweet retired Solitude . . . with her best nurse Contemplation") alongside *Richard III* 3.7.94: "So sweet is zealous contemplation." *Teares of the Muses*, 524–26; *Amoretti* 80, 10–11; and *Hymne to Heavenly Beautie*, 1–5, all have combinations of "sweet" and "contemplation." Every time Milton uses "faery" or "aery," Guillory seems to posit a reminiscence of *MND*. Paul Stevens uses the same words to explore the importance of *MND* and *Tempest* to Milton's epic in his refutation of Guillory.[22] In some cases Milton's alteration of words in earlier versions has given rise to implications of later obscuring to avoid plagiarism. "Comus" 117–18 ("And on the tawny Sands and Shelves,/Trip the pert Fairies and dapper Elves") had been "yellow Sands," and so Verity commented: "He wrote yellow, and perhaps changed to avoid too obvious comparison with Ariel's song," which is "Come unto these yellow sands." For Thaler the source was *MND* 2.1.125–26 ("she . . . sat with me on Neptune's yellow sands"). The *Aeneid*, the *Metamorphoses*, *Hero and Leander*, *Britannia's Pastorals* all have their share of yellow sands, among others.

Another kind of parallel is seen in the rhythm and structure of a line. In illustration of accentuation of "Lycidas," 165 ("Weep no more, woful Shepherds weep no more"), Keightley and Browne both cited *Much Ado* 2.3.65 ("Sign no more, ladies, sign no more"). Verity offered this for comparison, but Thaler indicated possible affinity. This pastoral convention is heard in a number of poems, but I think of an elegy in Wright and Halliwell's

John Milton and Influence

Reliquiae Antiquae (2.39): "Wep no more for me, swethart,/Wep no more for me!" Of *Samson Agonistes*, 1699–1707, Tillyard wrote: "And when the chorus speaks of the Phoenix they fall (whether with voluntary or involuntary reminiscence I do not know) into the metre and style of *The Phoenix and the Turtle* (lines 1–8)." Analyzing these passages one finds that the lines of *Phoenix* all have seven syllables, the first foot usually being an anapest, followed by two iambs; and that those of *SA* have 7, 8, 7, 8, 8, 11, 6, 10, and 9 syllables, the two seven-syllabled lines consisting of an anapest and two iambs. However, in *SA*, 606–16, as a random example, the syllabification is 9, 7, 8, 6, 7, 5, 10, 8, 7, 9, 6, the three seven-syllabled lines again consisting of an anapest and two iambs. Milton's meter when he talks of the phoenix is but the irregular meter he uses throughout the poem, apparently owing nothing to *The Phoenix and the Turtle*.

Often passages are fabricated from different lines in order to afford a parallel; for example, Grant McColley[23] conjoined lines 254–55, 276–78, and 282–83 of *PL* 6, and called *Macbeth* 5.8.3,6–7 their source:

He . . . oppos'd . . . his	*Macduff.* Turn, hell-hound,
ample Shield . . . to . . .	turn! . . . I have no words:
Hell . . . Ere this avenging	My voice is in
Sword . . . Nor think	my sword.
thou with wind . . . to aw	

Surely no one will contend appropriations of "Hell" and "sword" from Shakespeare; and Michael's "airie threats" are not Macbeth's "my soul is too much charged/With blood of thine already." It is evident that Satan's and Macduff's meanings are quite different: Satan calls Michael's words but meaningless boasts; Macduff, because of the circumstances and his emotions, cannot talk: he can only act.

An example of a similar invalid parallelism is the alleged source for "Comus," 307–10, [79], which Seaton found in *Romeo* 1.4.112, 2.2.82–84, 5.3.117:

To find out that [this adventurous glade], good Shepherd, I suppose, In such a scant allowance of Star-light,/Would overtask the best Land-Pilots art,/ Without the sure guess of well-practiz'd feet.	The steerage of my course, . . . I am no pilot; yet . . . I would adventure, . . . desperate pilot.

Just what Shakespearean reminiscences are supposed to be illustrated here is uncertain. There are only the words *pilot* and *adventrous/adventure*, but the two Shakespeare words come from different sections.

Another common method of the commentators is to use many Miltonic passages alongside a single Shakespearean "source" or many Shakespearean "sources" for a single Miltonic passage. Warton cited *MND* 2.1.6–7, 4.1.101–00, and *Macbeth* 3.5.23–24; Verity, *MND* 2.1.175; and Seaton, *Tempest* 4.1.76–83 as sources for "Comus," 1012–17. Likenesses are the ability to cover the earth and soar to the moon and the words "corners of the Moon," which is Ovid's "cornua lunæ."

A final way in which parallelism is created is by taking a passage or individual lines out of context. Thaler adduced *Cymbeline* 2.2.12–50 as Milton's model for dramatic hints for *PL* 9.457–69; but in addition to obscuring the situations of the passages by such excerpting, he afforded a further erroneous interpretation by omitting lines 468 and 470 of *PL*. Satan refers to the hell within him, which tortures him more when he sees pleasures not ordained for him because of this hell—in this instance, the pleasures of woman. He has spied Eve as she goes about her chores alone and comments on her angelic quality. Iachimo, Tarquin–like, desires to ravish the sleeping Imogen, but he is fearful of this lustful act: antithetically, though Imogen is a heavenly angel, ravishment of her would betake the ravisher to hell. Not only are these not equivalent dramatically, but the description of Eve has nothing in common with remarks made by Iachimo upon observing Imogen.

The foregoing illustrations of different kinds of methods of parallelism—equating seemingly unusual words, seizing upon manuscript alterations to maintain awareness of debt, equating literary constructions, fabricating either Miltonic or Shakespearean passages from numerous unrelated lines, juxtaposing a number of passsages from one against one passage from the other, and discussing passages out of context—define most of the alleged parallels advanced to establish Milton's debt to Shakespeare.

These parallels fall into five major divisions: those using similar language, those exhibiting similar thought, those presenting similar language and similar thought, those employing like image, and those showing dramatic likeness. I present just a few examples in each category, ones that have been fairly frequent and generally accepted.[24]

SIMILAR LANGUAGE

L'Allegro, 23–24/*Pericles* 1. Prologue.23 (Bowles). Likeness: "so bucksom, blith, and." Analogues: *FQ* 1.2.23; *Hero and Leander* 1.287–88; *Anatomy of Melancholy*, "Author's Abstract"; Aristippus, p. 21.

Comus, 11/*Measure* 1.4.34 (Gilchrist); *Antony* 1.3.28 (Verity), Likeness: "enthron'd gods on Sainted seats"/"ensky'd and sainted" and "throned gods."

PARALLELS OF THOUGHT

PL 11.685–92/*Coriolanus* 2.2.87–89 (George Coffin Taylor). Likeness: Valour is the greatest virtue. But Milton does not actually call valor the greatest virtue; he says that might in the past was admired and called valor, and it was considered the "highest pitch of human Glorie." The thought, of course, is not uncommon.

Defensio secunda (Columbia 8.6)/*Caesar* 3.2.35 (G. Wilson Knight). Likeness: "Who loves not his country?" Analogues: *Cornelia* 4.1.63–65, 4.2.116; *2 Tamburlaine* 5.1.4122–26.

Samson, 667 ff.; PL 7.505–11/*Hamlet* 2.2.316–23 (Thaler). Likeness: questioning of God's usage of humans and of their being the paragon of animals. Analogues: Job 7.17; Psalms 8.3, 4; Crashaw, *Charitas Nimia,* 1–4 (all ask the same question); *Metamorphoses* 1.76–88; *De Naturam Deorum* 2.56; Quarles, *Emblems* 3.5.3–30, 3.8.31–38 (all present both the question and the thought).

PARALLELS OF LANGUAGE AND THOUGHT

Lycidas, 134–51 (see also *Song,* 3–4)/*MND* 2.1.14–15, 249–52; (Thaler), 2.1.107–108, 128–29 (Verity); *2 Henry VI* 3.2.62–63 (Verity); *Winter's Tale* 4.4.105–106 (Verity), 122–24 (Newton); *Two Noble Kinsmen* 2.2 (pp. 312–13) (Verity); *Richard II* 3.3.47 (Whalley), 5.2.46–47 (Warton); *Cymbeline* 4.2.220–21 (Warton); *Henry V* 5.2.48–49 (V. R.). Likeness: 1) flower catalog (cowslip, violet, woodbine, muskrose); 2) "fresh lap," "wanton winds, "throw . . . green terf," "green lap"; 3) *Song* and Trinity MS reading of line 142–43 giving "pale," "primrose," "unwedded dies." Analogues: 1) *Shepheardes Calender,* Aprill, 55–63, 136–44; *Britannia's Pastorals* 2.3.351–411; Robinson, *Life and Death of Mary Magdalene,* 311–58, among many others. 2) *FQ* 2.6.15, 7.7.34; *Britannia's Pastorals* 2.3.1125–26; Herrick, *The Vision,*

11–12. 3) *A Sonnet of the Sun*, No. 230 in *Poetical Rhapsody*; Drayton, *Eglog* 9.9–12; *Shepherd's Pipe* 4.109–12; *Christ's Victorie on Earth* 59; Edmund Bolton, *Palinode* in *England's Helicon*; Carew, *Boldness in Love*. Henry H. Adams assigned Milton's corrections within the "Lycidas" passage to his realization of "plagiarism" of Perdita's catalogue. Some of the paralleling is strained; for example, Shakepeare's "And hang a pearl in every cowslip's ear" and Milton's "With cowslips wan that hang the pensive head," and Shakespeare's "freckled cowslip" and "Milton's "the Pansie freakt with jeat" (closer is Giles Fletcher's "The speckled pancie").

PL 12.492–95/*Macbeth* 5.8.30–31, 17–18 (Whalley, Dunster); *Henry V* 4.6.30–32 (Whalley, Newton, Dunster); *Macbeth* 1.3.139–41 (Seymour); *Hamlet* 4.7.186–90 (Verity). Likenesses: "not of Woman born"; "His best of Man"; "gave him up to tears." The last is most commonplace; the middle phrase is paralleled with "my better part of man," and is also commonplace. Of the first—"Though not of Woman born" and "being of no woman born"— Merritt Y. Hughes noted, "Here the reminiscence of *Macbeth* . . . must have been conscious," an unbelievable statement surely. Macduff is here being symbolized as a Christ figure, with his birth by Caesarean section suggesting a nonnormal birth like Jesus's miraculous birth. Adam, of course, was not of woman born, but by the miracle of God inspiriting the dust. There is nothing consciously remembered in Milton's lines. What Milton is doing, clearly, is paradoxically indicating that Adam, though not with female parentage, is nonetheless exhibiting an alleged stereotypical action of the female, crying. It is part of Milton's building-up of the importance of the female in achievement of redemption: Adam has been influenced by Eve, until "firmer thoughts restrained excess," where Milton now plays upon the stereotypical male attribute of firm mind over female emotion. (Such stereotyping creates unhappiness for us, but it is there in *Paradise Lost*, although that does not mean that Milton accepted it, and it exists in most people's thinking even today.)

PARALLELS OF IMAGE

(primarily Imagery of Night, Imagery of Day, and Imagery of Folklore)

PL 1. 789–88/*MND* 2.1.28–29, 141 (Callander); *Tempest* 2.4.4–5 (anonymous). Likeness: fairy antics and dance. Douglas Bush in *Mythology and the Renaissance Tradition* expressed the belief that "A fairy dance is unexpected in *Paradise Lost*, and it is to another of Milton's favorite plays that we turn for suggestions" (referring to *MND*). There are numerous analogues, but note as well Pliny's *Natural History* 7.2.25–26, and *Batman upon Bartholomew*, p. 377, and see Stevens for further discussion.

PARALLELS OF DRAMATIC LIKENESS

PR 2.236–39, 340–67, 401–03/*Tempest* 4.1.35, 3.3.17–19 and direction, 3.3.52 and direction (Thaler, but see Peck, p. 207). There is a major difference between Satan's invitation to eat and the disappearance of the banquet, and invitations by the strange shapes and Ariel's making the banquet

25

vanish: Satan wants the Son to eat, but when he refuses the temptation, it is no longer necessary and it disappears; Prospero does not want Alonzo and his party to eat but merely wishes to taunt them, and when they seem about to partake, after a discussion of the phenomenal appearance of the feast, he has the banquet vanish. The evil intent of beguiling in *PR* is similar to Cleopatra's banquet for Caesar in Lucan's account (10.111–71, particularly 155–58). Satan's "tall stripling youths" are neither devils in disguise nor the equivalents of "several strange shapes" who bring in the banquet, dance, and make offers to have the king eat: they are the attendants at a sumptuous feast. The harmonious airs played at Satan's banquet are but the accompanying music necessary for good digestion (see "Lawrence of virtuous Father"and Epicurean works). Prospero's "solemn and strange music" calls the group's attention to the banquet and provides the music for the strange shapes to dance to. In Shakepeare the music comes first, followed by the banquet and then the dancing shapes; in Milton the chosen band accompanies Satan to do what he wishes well before the banquet is created, the luxuriant table is manned by richly clad serving boys, in the distance are nymphs who "now dance, now solemn stand," and soothing music quite unlike Prospero's is heard all the while. It seems to me that the stage-setting is quite different in the two works, and that Milton is closest to *Godfrey of Bulloigne* 10.64, where there is a disappearance of the banquet. The references to harpies constitute but a matter of common belief about them, as given in *Aeneid* 3.223–28.

There are, therefore, no unique likenesses between

Milton's and Shakespeare's banquets. Nonetheless Thaler's remark is in opposition: "The feast in *Paradise Regained,* prepared by Satan to tempt Christ, in its stage-setting, and in the final disposition made of it distinctly resembles that prepared by Ariel for the shipwrecked mariners, according to the stage directions of the First Folio .... Milton's stage-setting, at all events (the music, dance, and the rest), is closer to Shakspere than to Tasso, and Tasso says nothing of the disappearance of the banquet with the flapping of the harpies' wings at the end."

We should note that Warton equated the stage direction in "Comus" (658–59) with the same *Tempest* stage direction. But the scene change in the masque is from a part of the forest to Comus's palace, the foods laid out are to be not only an inducement for the Lady to submit to him, but also to allow him to offer her the magic potion. See for Miltonic similarity the description of Armida's feast in *Gerusalemme Liberata* 10.61–65.

What seems to have happened over the years is that commentators have hoped that there was an extensive relationship between the two great British authors. Both of these authors have been read more extensively and intensively than others, and this seems to have led to the often gross paralleling of the language, ideas, and devices of the common stock of poetry. The parallels are almost always from familiar works and from continuous familiar lines within those works. In *Paradise Lost,* for instance, it will be noted that certain books have a tremendous number of "parallels," whereas others are relatively untouched. These books are the most well known and most often referred to in criticism: 1, 2, 4, 9, and 10. The most familiar plays of Shakespeare and most familiar passages within those plays are used to formulate the literary debt. Very often the same passage or contiguous passages are used to illustrate reminiscence in various Miltonic works: *MND* 2.1 provides 43 "parallels," for instance.

The point is twofold: the source-seekers find those lines and passages in Shakespeare that are memorable to them in lines and passages from Milton that are likewise memorable to them; further, Milton's own repetition of like language or thought within his own writings is paralleled over and over with the same Shakespearean passages, thus swelling the number of "reminiscences." On this basis, it has been said that Milton's "familiarity with the poems and plays can be verified by a glance at any annotated edition of Milton's poems," and that "Milton's eager reading of the plays is well attested."[25] In view of the results of my study, I think we must question the intent of such remarks as J. W. Hales's: "The subject of 'Paradise Lost' is the ruin of man; and what else is the subject of 'Macbeth'?" where he seems not to understand Lady Macbeth and Macbeth as infernal Eve and Adam killing their Lord, so that they might become like him. It is not a matter of literary debt; it is a matter of working in the same subject and tradition. Or Taylor's assertion that *Samson Agonistes*, which he says corresponds to a long fifth act, gives more convincing evidence than anything else Milton wrote that the influence of Shakespeare was increasing rather than decreasing (he of course dates *Samson Agonistes* last of the poems) and that this influence, most obviously from *Troilus*, accounts in part for the form.

If Milton did read Shakespeare extensively, if certain verbal, figurative, or dramatic passages stayed with Milton, and if he used this possible reminiscence in his own work, consciously or unconsciously, it cannot be ascertained by the "parallels" that have generally been offered. As I said before, it is impossible to prove, for the most part, that one writer did not remember another, but as the suggested remembrances have been seen to be commonplace or nonexistent, that reminiscence is suspect, and no statement of debt can be inferred.

The questions to be faced—but after all the meaningless demonstrations of the critics' remembrances of Shakespeare and Milton and when source-hunting is no longer a goal—are, how did Shakespeare affect Milton's poetic voice? What elements in Milton's verse indicate allusive employment of Shakespeare? And what elements are echoes of Shakespeare? That one author may reflect another consciously and unconsciously should not be used as scaffolding for some high-flown thesis of the later author's paucity of expression or thought or struggled rejection of the other. The effect of such a high-flown thesis can be seen in Guillory's book, where, in Bloomian determinism, the author argues that Milton's rejection of Shakespeare arises from an opposition of sacred poetry's revelation of God's creation to an imaginative secular poetry created from no externally inspired source. The opposition is worked largely through "Comus" and *Paradise Lost*, and *Midsummer Night's Dream* and *The Tempest*, and the reading he posits of Milton's poems reflects a superficial restatement of Milton as member of Satan's party. Possibly all I am saying is that the book is thesis-ridden, by which I mean that the thesis obliterates the author's investigation of other issues or elements in a determination to advance the thesis. The book's achievement lies in discussion of the significant way in which one author's poetic voice is influenced by another, as indeed I believe Milton's was by Spenser and by Shakespeare, though differently. Unfortunately that achievement is deflected by a thesis that is not cogent and is not built on a valid reading of Milton's work.

The most recent statement on Shakespeare and Milton, Paul Stevens's study, offers a counterview to Guillory's by examination largely of these same four works. The writings Stevens confines himself to are only ones allowing surface intertexts. He states, "it is the purpose of the present study to substantiate its central proposition, that imagination is the vehicle of faith, by explicating some of the more extensive patterns of Shakespearean echo and allusion . . . " (7). Stevens contrasts *mimesis phantastike* (that is, fancy), the imitation of unnatural things synthesized in the mind from disparate parts of the real world, and *mimesis eikastike*, the imitation of natural actions and things as they commonly appear in the world. He thus attempts to confute Guillory's basic reading and extrapolation of "On Shakespear." Neither book, in terms of Milton's literary debt to Shakespeare, goes much beyond Percy Allen, unnoted by either, or Ethel Seaton, employed by Stevens only, in their examinations of these same four works, in terms of demonstrable echoes, al-though they do not manufacture echoes as Allen and Seaton do. Both books are given over to a critical position rather than a historically critical assessment of Milton's debt to Shakespeare, a study yet to be engaged.

The terms *allusion* and *echo* are, of course, difficult to define with exactitude, as most paired terms are—even *secular* and *sacred*. Paired terms at their extremes can be defined, but most of the time the reality lies between those extremes: like black and white, and good and evil. By *allusion*, I mean a conscious employment of a reference or of words or lines or image or characterization or setting to evoke a remembrance from the reader. The purpose in using an allusion is to add meaning, for the allusion will bring to the fore a network of ideas or pictures from the source. An allusion may be positive, as with the epilogue of the Attendant Spirit in "Comus," whose "To the oceans now I fly" recalls Ariel in *The Tempest* and leads the reader to infer that a chapter in some persons' lives has been completed, with instruction for future action. The audience or readers may be so instructed, too, to follow virtue and to believe in the efficacy of supernal forces. This allusion suggests that Milton read *The Tempest* with some degree of allegoric understanding, Prospero becoming a godlike magus and Miranda and Ferdinand the instructed influences for a better world, just as the lady and, to an extent, her brothers are. "List, mortals, if your ears be true," the Spirit says, and so somewhat didactically Milton insinuates himself into the masque, obliquely addressing the audience.[26] Shakespeare's governmental disquisition is not, of course, so obvious. "To the oceans now I fly" may be echo, but it becomes allusion for the reader recognizing the echo, and thus suggests conscious use by Milton.

An allusion may be critical, implying a subtle revision of what might first have been understood; as, for example, when in *Fanny Hill* the voyeurs observe a supposed virgin coyly fending off a new, handsome master—in contrast with her rather extensive experience—and he takes her hand to lead her to a couch and she goes *nothing loth.*[27] John Cleland is alluding to Eve just after the Fall in book 9 of *Paradise Lost*, when Adam seizes her hand in lust. At the beginning of the book their usual hand-in-hand description is broken by Eve's withdrawing her hand, and the temptation and fall then proceed. Adam leads Eve to the sexual lustfulness described just before the book ends, and Eve goes *nothing loth.* Milton's poetry evokes a description of *fallen* woman as playing coy in such seduction, but who, being fallen, really wants to engage in such sexual activity, which is so differently described for both the man and the woman in book 4 before the Fall. Cleland

31

is letting his reader see Louisa as a daughter of the fallen Eve, and the allusion curtails any thought that Louisa could be even slightly coy as she has really been leading on her master, just as the superficial and male-oriented reading of the scene in *Paradise Lost* would argue that Eve has been the cause of Adam's fall. (That is, of course, an entirely different subject from this essay's, but we should understand that Adam is the cause of his own fall; it is only Eve who is tempted by Satan).

By *echo*, I mean an unconscious appearance of words or lines or image, that is, unconscious to the author when the author wrote, but possibly this is subconscious. Echo has two major significations: it may create an allusion for the reader; or it may provide analysis of what the author was more fully concerned with, thus describing an author's "intertextual mind." It may focus the elements that have been deeply impressive for that author.[28] But to move an echo to authorial allusion should be demonstrated for each alleged allusion. An example is Milton's use of a line from Giles Fletcher in Eve's description of her dream in book 5, which has been cited in the past as what we would now label echo but which I have argued is purposive allusion, bringing in for the informed reader a proleptic view of the Fall.[29] Many remembrances lie in-between allusion and echo as I have defined them, and that is one reason why much difference of opinion will enter as to Milton's debt to Shakespeare. One must, at least generally, take each seeming remembrance separately to see whether it is allusion or echo or a seemingly unconscious echo which instead can be demonstrated to be a very subtle allusion. I conclude with an example of each of these.

In a study of Ovid and Milton, Richard J. Du Rocher is wisely concerned with the dialogue between the two authors: "Milton," he writes, "repeatedly invokes yet criticizes Ovid while inviting the earlier poet to act upon, even to transform his epic argument."[30] The Renaissance term for the process was *emulatio,* and it is that emulation of Milton for Shakespeare—that dialogue that is created—that more properly offers an assessment of Milton's debt to Shakespeare.

In his last sonnet, "Methought I saw my late espoused saint," Milton relates a dream in which his dead wife approached him only to disappear (or dissolve) as she inclined to embrace him: "my late espoused saint . . ./Came vested all in white, pure as her mind." Such a theme of resurrection is common doubly to *The Winter's Tale* and is focal to the mythological substruct of the death of nature in winter and its rejuvenation in spring. Perdita and Hermione are restored to Leontes in act 5: the myth of Persephone, being emphasized in Perdita's association with flowers and with Florizel, paves the way for the "resurrection" of the wife Hermione. But at the center of the play, in act 3, scene 3, Antigonus remarks, "I have heard, but not believed, the spirits of the dead/May walk again, and relates Hermione's appearance to him in a dream the night before; after her message is given, "with shrieks,/ She melted into thin air." Hermione's appearance is described in language and situation that Milton may have unconsciously echoed in his sonnet (first noted by Walker, 3: 103):

> To me comes a creature,
> Sometimes her head on one side, some another,
> I never saw a vessel of like sorrow,
> So filled and so becoming. In pure white robes
> Like very sanctity, she did approach
> My cabin where I lay, thrice bowed before me,
> And, gasping to begin some speech, her eyes
> Became two spouts.

At the end of her message to him, she informs Antigonous that

> For this ungentle business,
> Put on thee by my lord, thou ne'er shalt see
> Thy wife Paulina more.

The situation is certainly suggestive of echo, and if it were subconsciously in Milton's mind, emerging as he dreamed of his dead wife, we may have an example of religious questioning on Milton's part. Does indeed resurrection occur, or is it just in fleeting moments of light midst darkness that hope of return can rise only to be dashed by reality? For as the vision inclined to embrace him, he awakened and the vision fled. Dreams, of course, seldom allow for the consummation of action, and the sonnet pictures that reality. But the poem, ranging as it does over pagan, Hebraic, and Christian hopes of salvation, poses more for the reader than only a retelling of a dream and one man's desire for return. The subject becomes less "On his deceased wife," a title given the poem in 1721 by Elijah Fenton, than it does humankind's persistent belief in resurrection and salvation to shore one against the realness of finality. Antigonus, of course, goes into the night of death and nevermore sees Paulina, and Perdita and Hermione mythically illustrate the observation of nature's yearly renewal, the source of resurrectional fictions.

Echo that may become allusion seems to exist in the Attendant Spirit's opening lines of "A Mask" ("Comus"):

> Neptune . . . Took in . . .
> Imperial rule of all the Sea-girt Iles
> That like to rich and various gems inlay
> The unadorned bosom of the deep . . .
>
> (18–23)

Although Phineas Fletcher's *The Purple Island* II, 16, tells of "a sea [which] girts th'Isle in every port," John of Gaunt's apostrophe to England affords various language and image echoes, which may then suggest more significance:

> This royal throne of kings, this scepter'd isle,
> . . . this little world,
> This precious stone set in the silver sea, . . .
>
> (*Richard II* 2.1.40–46)

These lines were paralleled by Newton and Warton. Milton emphasizes the maritime relationships of the British isle, moving to Wales, whose presidency by John Egerton, the Earl of Bridgewater, was being officially celebrated. "This Ile/The greatest and the best of all the main" Neptune "quarters to his blu-haired deities." The praise of Britain, which Gaunt calls "This earth of majesty, This seat of Mars,/This other Eden, demi-Paradise," is "The envious seige/Of watery Neptune, . . . now bound in with shame,/With inky blots and rotten parchment bonds." "Ah, would the scandal vanish with my life," he laments (41–42, 62–64).

The circumstances of Gaunt's regrets for what has occurred in England and a context furnishing background for the Bridgewater event and Milton's mask of chastity are quite different, of course, but in Gaunt's lines there can be a curious reminder of the Castlehaven scandal, involving Bridgewater's brother-in-law, whose sexual aberrations must have been on the audience's minds as they heard lines about "carnal sensuality . . . link't . . . To a degenerate and degraded state." Those in Milton's audience (and now modern readers), recognizing echoes of *Richard II*, would understand as allusion the corruption of state and person by flattery and the love of pleasure: perhaps

Milton's message is as much advice to the new Lord President as it is more generally to "Mortals . . . [to] Love Vertue." The mask is a first examination of the temptation in the wilderness, and suggests, by its echoing *Richard II* and the possible allusion thereunto, that each small, individual resistance of temptation may accrue to a more momentous resistance of corruption in high places.

We have already noted the infamy of Richard III, a reputed tyrant and evil personification. Such lines as those toward the close of the play find analogues in other contemporary literature:

> What do I fear? Myself? There's none else by:
> Richard loves Richard; that is, I am I.
> Is there a murderer here? No. Yes, I am.
> Then fly. What, from myself? Great reason why:
> Lest I revenge. What, myself upon myself?
> (5.3.182–86)

> Swift from myself I run, myself I fear,
> Yet still my hell within myself I bear.
> (*Godfrey of Bulloigne* 12.17)

> Where may I fly into some desert place,
> Some uncouth, unfrequented craggy rocke,
> Where as my name and state was never heard.
> (*Caesar's Revenge* 1.1.61–63)

> Whither fly I? To that place can I safely fly? to which mountain? to what den? to what strong house? what castle shall I hold? what wall should hold me? Wither soever I go, myself followeth me: For whatsoever thou fliest, O man, thou mayst, but thy own conscience . . .
> (Quarles, St. Augustine's *Psalm 33*)

One's self cannot be abandoned: one is who one is. And thus the evil Richard has done defines himself: "I am I," with perhaps a glance, demanding dialectic understanding, at the Lord's "I am that I am."

A clear analogue to this depiction of conscience, particularly the conscience of evil seen in the above, is the presentation of Satan and his soliloquy in book 4 of *Paradise Lost:*

> The Hell within him, for within him Hell
> He brings, and round about him, nor from Hell
> One step no more then from himself can fly . . .
> Which way I flie is Hell; myself am Hell.
> (*PL* 4.20–22, 75; cited by G. C. Taylor)

While Milton may not have meant to allude directly and only to Richard in the character of Satan,[31] the characterization falls into the same type, and the similarity of thought and language etches that type into the reader's awareness. For the reader, Milton has provided a dialogue, whether intentionally or unintentionally, between Shakespeare's deformed and psychologically impaired protagonist and Satan: both observe sexual joys not fully available to them; both bring themselves to their evil deeds by pride and a belief in a lack of deserving love. The reader may see Richard through such a comparison even more as one bewailing his natural being so that it becomes the cause for his deformity of character; Satan's reaction to the new statement of God's supremacy through the delineation of another aspect of God, the Son—who nonetheless is God as before, with Satan in no different relationship to godhead—as one unaccepting of things as they are.

The dialogue that Milton sets up by the allusion to Richard—or, if not by direct allusion, by the placement of Satan in the world of tyrannic malcontents—is to emphasize that evil within creates a hell within, never to be altered unless that evil be expelled. In contrast, of course, are Eve and Adam who, prior to the Fall, had neither hell nor paradise within themselves, but who, instructed, have the opportunity at the end of the epic to develop a paradise within that is happier far. Some, however, like Cain or Nimrod, will emulate the Richards of this world. The allusion, whether Milton's or ours, the readers', works to give depth of character and meaning to both Shakespeare and Milton.

How does Shakespeare affect Milton's poetic voice? My earlier discussions deny the mere repetition of Shakespearean language and argue the placement of both authors in the same poetic traditions. Milton did not learn his poetic, imaged vocabulary from Shakespeare, though he might echo him from time to time. Like all of us, Milton would have been struck by Shakespeare's language, images, aptness of phrase, rhythms, characterizations, narrative elements, contrasts and comparisons, and memorable statements of ordinary ideas. People knowing nothing of Shakespeare may, as the occasion makes pertinent, talk of "What's in a name?" and we, feeling down in the dumps because we were passed over for that meaningful appointment, might solace ourselves with "When in disgrace with fortune and men's eyes." At times such remembrances may have emerged in Milton's work from the more prominent use of *The Tempest* in "A Mask" to the more subtle reference to Caesar's spirit crying havoc and letting slip the dogs of war in the Dogs of Hell that advance to waste and havoc the world.[32] But my study of these two authors places then at a good distance from each other, and I cannot conclude that Milton's poetic voice was greatly affected by Shakespeare's or that he felt pangs of anxiety over the "easier numbers" and imagination of the world's greatest dramatist.

TWO

Criterion of Taste and Source of Knowledge: Milton in Some Lesser Known Eighteenth Century Places

T he second edition of *Paradise Lost* in 1674 apparently did not sell so well as most people would like to think. There was a reissue in 1675, which is noted by Francis Blackburne in his *Remarks on Johnson's Life of Milton* (1780) in an addendum chronologically listing Milton's publications. The only known copy of this reissue is housed in the University of Illinois Library. The implication of this evidence is that Milton was well received by only a relatively small group of readers. A new edition came out in 1678, but it was not until the fourth edition in 1688 that Milton's reputation finally rose sharply. This edition, although it is often associated with Lord Somers, who was one of the subscribers, was apparently the result of effort by Francis Atterbury, Henry Aldrich and a group at Christ Church, Cambridge. Probably Somers's high position was used to advance the cause of the edition.

The volume is among the first English poems published with illustrations, most of which were by Sir John Baptista de Medina, but also by Bernard Lens and Aldrich. It was one of the first published by subscription, and Dryden is included, as is Milton's sometime antagonist in governmental areas, Sir Roger L'Estrange. A November 1687 letter from Atterbury to Jacob Tonson, one of the publishers, is extant and discusses the venture; it gives a list of subscribers, and is now in the Folger Shakespeare Library. The edition had three issues, with three different title pages, and is found on heavy paper and ordinary paper, with and without gilt edges. It is an impressive book.

A vindication of the poem in Charles Gildon's *Miscellaneous Letters and Essays, on Several Subjects* (1694) was directed to a Mr. T. S., who remains unidentified; an erratum gives the author as I. I. But what that means one cannot be sure; Gildon has also been credited with its authorship. However, in that volume Gildon did answer Thomas Rymer in "Some Reflections on Mr. Rymer's Short View of Tragedy," alluding twice to Milton's blank verse favorably, even though Rymer had not mentioned Milton in this volume. Rymer's half line in "Tragedies of the Last Age" (1678) not only registered with Dryden, who alluded to it in "Original and Progress of Satire," *The Satires of Decimus Junius Juvenalis* (1693), but also, for example, with Thomas Shipman, who in *Henry the Third of France* (1678) disavows Milton's blank verse and says he will not add further discussion because Rymer is going to show its inadequacies.

This then is the background out of which eighteenth century poets and critics came to read and react to Milton's epic: a growing but discriminating audience, some of whom reacted favorably and some most unfavorably to its prosody. Yet if cultural opinions are stated often enough, they seep down to others who either are curious to see for themselves or are satisfied to repeat dicta when their pertinence arises, and Milton's presence in the century following his death looms large.

In a lecture to the British Academy in 1908, Edward Dowden began,

> The influence of Milton on the literature of the eighteenth century was threefold—an influence on poetic style, independent in a great degree of poetic matter . . . ; secondly, an influence alike on sentiment and style . . . ; thirdly, an influence on thought, appearing at irregular intervals, but always associated with political liberalism or radicalism . . . . The first of these modes of influence is chiefly connected with *Paradise Lost*, the second with Milton's earlier poems, the third with his prose writings.[1]

John W. Good detailed some of the evidence of this threefold influence in 1915 in *Studies in the Milton Tradition*,[2] and George Sherburn made clear in his essay "The Early Popularity of Milton's Minor Poems"[3] that the second influence was more widespread and frequent than we had been led to believe from statements made by Thomas Warton and others. A fair amount of work has been published on Miltoniana during the century, such as Raymond Dexter Havens's study of *The Influence of Milton on English Poetry*[4] with its long lists of imitative works (usually of *Paradise Lost*, "L'Allegro," and "Il Penseroso") and of borrowings. My own epitome of this topic stated:

> The first part of the eighteenth century saw an intensified continuation of the evaluation of Milton and his works which had evolved during the 1690s. The Miltonic tradition of the man, the philosopher, and the artist was

established by 1731. Most often Milton's "sublimity" was asserted: by this commentators meant the capacity of his poetry to enlarge the imagination of his readers. . . . [However,] during the period 1700–31, in addition to a tacit objection to Milton's politics, there was fault-finding with the ideas and characters, literary devices, language, and prosody of *Paradise Lost.*[5]

Milton criticism from 1732 to 1801 may be divided into four periods dominated by certain critics or concerns. But such divisions are specious, for the 70 years of the eighteenth century move through all the areas of Milton criticism explored in the years prior to 1732.[6]

The four periods to which I refer in this latter comment are 1732–1740, with its textual criticism, ushered in by Richard Bentley in 1732, and an accompanying attention to language, explication, and style, and with its religious controversy, initiated really in 1698 by John Toland's *Life of John Milton,* but reemergent in 1738 as an argument over the alleged Arianism of *Paradise Lost.* Second, 1741–1751, when praise and analysis are countered by some dispraise and disparagement, largely at the hands of William Lauder, but leading to a fuller examination of Milton's sources. Third, 1752–1773, a period that does not see "a new turn in Milton criticism or offer any single dominant concern" (30), since it airs both defense against adverse critics and analyzes anew the poems, language, versification, style, and so forth. Fourth, 1774–1801, a period that produced some outstanding criticism of Milton (some like James Burnet, Lord Monbaddo's being little known today), with its closer analysis of the man, his life, and many of his works, plus an increasing number of editions and translations. "As the century ends, Milton is more entrenched in the position he held in 1732: he is still the exemplar of sublime thought and expression, he is widely imitated and quoted, and he is employed as authority for idea and language or for poetic licence," as I have previously remarked (33).

This epitome I shall demonstrate here, but rather than look at such obvious evidence as the work of Edward Young or William Mason or William Cowper, or the critical views of Lord Kames or Joseph Warton or William Hayley, I shall cite a number of lesser known authors or sources to indicate that Milton is, in the eighteenth century, a criterion of taste and a source of knowledge for the more average person, the average person who indeed might not have read Milton very extensively but who is reflecting the tenor of the times. It has often been observed that one can learn more about the culture of a historical period by looking at the lesser writers, at the ordinary people of the times. Undoubtedly, Robert Ludlum's *The Aquitaine Progression* or George Gipe's *Gremlins* is a better index of mid-1984 reading habits than is Muriel Spark's *The Only Problem* or Barbara Pym's diary and letters, *A Very Private Eye*. What I find as I move through eighteenth century publications is that Milton does loom large as a given, a presence that does not have to be explained or detailed or justified. Of necessity my remarks are going to be fairly bibliographic, but the conclusion will be clear even if the details are less than memorable.

Currently there is no bibliography of Milton and Miltoniana for the eighteenth century. Some of the items already mentioned, as well as William Riley Parker's *Milton: A Biography* and Kathleen Coleridge's *A Descriptive Catalogue of the Milton Collection in the Alexander Turnbull Library*, supply the start for such a compilation. Most of the items that I shall note have not previously been cited in Milton studies.

In 1785, the year Thomas Warton published the first edition of his influential *Poems Upon Several Occasions by John Milton* and brought forth Samuel Darby's *A Letter to the Rev. Mr. T. Warton*, which attacked Warton's editorial policy, the *European Magazine* printed 18 significant items having an association with Milton. In 1785 as well, in London there appeared two editions of *Paradise Lost* and one from Kilmarnock, one two-volume and one one-volume reprint of Bishop Thomas Newton's *Paradise Regain'd* and the remaining poems, as well as various other incidental items, like "Adam's Morning Hymn" (*PL* 5.153–208), in Oliver Goldsmith's edition of *Poems For Young Ladies*, and the first collection of Samuel Johnson's poetical works with its "Prologue to Comus." (A complete listing for the year would also record an Italian translation of "L'Allegro" by Domenico Testa in Parma, a Russian translation of *Paradise Lost* from a French translation by Serebrennikov Amvrosii in Moscow, and a Russian translation of *Paradise Regain'd* from a French translation by Ivan Greshishchev, also in Moscow.) Allusions and discussions in rather obvious belletristic works that year are found in Hugh Blair's *Lectures on Rhetoric* (Edition 2, corrected), John Scott's *Critical Essays on Some of the Poems of Several English Poets*, William Cook's (?) *The Life of Samuel Johnson*, Joseph Richardson's enlargement of his *Criticism on the Rolliad*, Sir John Hawkins's *Probationary Odes for the Laureateship* and Robert Heron's (that is, John Pinkerton's) *Letters of Literature*. Heron, for example, quotes from various works—"Comus," Sonnet 12, *Paradise Regain'd*, *Paradise Lost*, "Il Penseroso"—and discusses such matters as Milton's spelling, pronunciation, and literary reputation, as well as epic and Milton's originality.

Imitations and poetic influences, of course, also could be seen in a new edition of Alexander Pope's poetical works published by Andrew Foulis in Glasgow, in David Garrick's poetical works, "Now First Collected into Two

Volumes," in Samuel Richardson's *Clarissa Harlowe* newly translated into French and published in Geneva, in the anonymous *The Beauties of the Brinsleiad,* and in Timothy Dwight's *The Conquest of Canaan.* But few readers will know Clara Reeve's *The Progress of Romance, Through Times, Countries, and Manners; with Remarks on the good and Bad Effects of it, on them respectively.* A discussion of Gothic imagery in volume 1 comes out of the example of Milton in the two epics and "Il Penseroso," and volume 2 gives us John Dryden's verses on Milton as critical epitome again. These verses had first been printed beneath Robert White's engraving of Milton in the milestone fourth edition of *Paradise Lost* in 1688.

In *Memoirs of the Literary and Philosophical Society of Manchester,* the first volume of which is dated 1785, we find (among other matters) the issue of blank verse again raised by Thomas Barnes in "On the Nature and Essential Characters of Poetry, as Distinguished from Prose," and Milton's poems are among the fountainheads for "An Essay on the Pleasures which the Mind Receives from the Exercise of Its Faculties, and that of Taste in particular," by Charles de Polier. Incidentally, one of de Polier's examples come from book 6 of *Paradise Lost,* that often maligned book, which even Marjorie Hope Nicolson pilloried in saying, "For the most part, the battles in Heaven seem fought by glorified tin soldiers."[7] In rebuttal we find the eighteenth century frequently citing and quoting book 6 as sublime, a thought beginning with the Earl of Roscommon's second edition of "An Essay on Translated Verse" (1685). Here Roscommon inserts an apostrophe to Milton's poem in blank verse (11. 377–403) into his poem, which otherwise is in heroic couplets, and notes in the margin book 6 as reference for the substance of his added lines. Further, we might note Thomas Reid's *Essays on the Intellectual Powers of Man,* which takes its content from *Paradise Lost* frequently; John Roberts's *The Belloniad, An Heroic Poem*, with numerous allusions, quotations, and imitations; Mary O'Brien's *The Pious Incendiaries: or, Fanaticism Display'd A Poem*, with reference on pp. 53, 55, 57; and Peter Williams's *Letters Concerning Education: Addressed to a Gentleman Entering the University* with its numerous references to and quotations from *Of Education, Paradise Lost*, and *Paradise Regain'd.*

During the latter part of the century, much attention was paid to language—grammar, punctuation, elocution, and the like—and Milton was frequently cited for his beauties of expression and style. He was largely an exemplar, as four books we can remark for 1785 attest. George Neville Usher in *The Elements of English Grammar, Methodically Arranged* uses *Paradise Lost* often (there were further editions in 1786, 1789, and 1796). Joseph Robertson also employed the epic for examples and springboards into discussion in *An Essay on Punctuation*. But John Walker, in *A Rhetorical Grammar, or Course of Lessons in Elocution*, not only does likewise but moves into fuller discussion of language matters (such as the ungrammatical use of *ye* and the linguistic effect of the particle *the*), into anastrophe, inflection, puns, and how to read simile. Yet one main concern is sublimity, its description and effect. Walker also takes the first 26 lines of *Paradise Lost*—that is, the proem up through "And justifie the ways of God to men"—and parallels them as written with a more prosaic revision to illustrate what blank verse is. While other authors are also used extensively in these language-oriented volumes—such as Pope and Johnson and, though perhaps surprisingly, Shakespeare less frequently—Milton certainly holds his own in a numbers game and generally outshines others as an exemplar or for the number of quotations from his poems used as starting points for a discussion.

I choose 1785 to mention for no particular reason: a year toward the end of the century but before the romantic swell of interest offers substance for my view that Milton's position then is even more entrenched than that which he held in the first part of the century. And 1785 is the year of William Cowper's *The Task* and the year after Johnson's death, but a date prior to William Blake's work, with the exception of the very Elizabethan *Poetical Sketches* in 1783. *The European Magazine* is frequently overlooked; certainly it has been in Milton scholarship, and yet in this one year there are 18 items worthy of attention as noted before. First, there is an anonymous "Account of the Writings of Dr. Samuel Johnson" (7:9–12, 82), which has numerous references to Milton and which reprints Garrick's poem on the dictionary. Parts of Richardson's critique on *The Rolliad* (7:43–50, 219–22), Heron's *Letters of Literature* (8:196), and the prefatory material to the probationary odes (8:75) appear in the periodical, certainly reaching a larger audience than the books themselves. Joseph Ritson refers to John Dalton's *Comus* in "Historical View of the Progress of English Song" (7:94), as does a review of *The Revenge of Guendolon* (7:275), and eight lines are reprinted in the frontispiece to volume 8. Letters to the Philological Society often refer to Milton (7:321), one alleging Pope's imitation of the "Nativity Ode" (7:413–14) and another criticizing John Baskerville's printing of *Paradise Lost*.

Anonymous, or seemingly anonymous, reviews in the magazine make casual remarks, thus suggesting Milton's primacy for those critics. One rejects Milton's indebtedness to Richard Crashaw's "Sospetto d'Herode" in a review of Peregrine Philips's edition (7:346). A review of Ann Yearsley's *Poems on Several Occasions* brought forth an allusion (8:116), and a review of Thomas Pennant's *Arctic Zoology*, a quotation from *Paradise Lost* (8:121). There is also a two-part, nine-page review of Warton's edition

(7:419–23; 8:32–35). Daniel Defoe's allusion to Milton in *The Groans of Great Britain* is quoted in a letter (7:418); and two sections of "Fragments by Leo" give a quotation from Shaftesbury on Milton (8:271) and a discussion of Milton's suffering at the hands of critics (8:334–35).

Some samples of Milton as a source of knowledge, in places for the most part that might not be expected and from various periods, are:

1) James Parsons uses *History of Britain* to examine early learning in the British Isles, in *Remains of Japhet: Being Historical Enquiries into the Affinity and Origin of the European Languages* (1767; pp. 142–43).

2) A writer in *Gentleman's Magazine* in 1739 (9:57), in an article titled, "A Demonstration that the Relations in Mr. Gulliver's Voyages are no fictions," verified the existence of pygmies by Milton's authority (see the end of book 1 of *Paradise Lost*).

3) Among various references and quotations, Henry Coventry employed Milton's verse to discuss conjugal life and wedded love in *Philemon to Hydaspes; Relating A Second Conversation with Hortensius upon the Subject of False Religion* (1737; pp. 40–44).

4) *The Pulpit and Family Bible. Containing, the Sacred Text of the Old and New Testaments at Large*, a learned volume with annotations, marginal notes, and parallel scriptures in Greek and Hebrew (Edinburgh, 1766), cites *Paradise Lost* 1.19–22 to explain Genesis 1.2.

5) For discussions of human faculties, imagination, freedom of choice, and providence, in *Essays Moral*

and Philosophical on Several Subjects (1734),
Alexander Forbes quotes Milton to support his
ideas.

Some books that instance Milton as a criterion of taste
and style are: Henry Felton's *A Dissertation on Reading
the Classics, and Forming a Just Style. Written in the Year
1709* (Ed. 4, 1730); Charles Lamotte's *An Essay Upon Poetry and Painting, with Relation to the Sacred and Profane
History* (1730), which, incidentally, discusses decorum
and license (110–12) by recourse to *Paradise Lost*; John
Constable's *Reflections upon Accuracy of Style* (1731);
and John Newbery's *The Art of Poetry on a New Plan*
(1762). This last, like most of the volumes noted, references or quotes *Paradise Lost* extensively, but also the
companion poems which were extremely popular during
the eighteenth century, and "Song: On May Morning."
Newbery notes Milton's importance to Thomas Gray's
"Elegy," Buckingham's "Essay on Poetry," Edward Young's
"Love of Fame, The Universal Passion," and Samuel
Garth's "The Dispensary."

An unpublished thesis by Gracie Lee Keeley in 1940
explored Milton's reputation in this century through the
Gentleman's Magazine and the *Monthly Review*. A series
of articles drawn from Nancy Lee-Riffe's unpublished
dissertation in 1963 of Milton's reputation in British
periodicals, 1711–88, led to the same conclusion: Milton
was well known and well quoted, and an authority figure.
As Lee-Riffe says in one essay: "In a period in which the
divorce tracts were virtually forgotten, Milton may have
been considered a misogynist by some, but for more he
seems to have been a kind of patron saint of marriage."[8]
Yet Morris Golden's article in the *Bulletin of the New
York Public Library* in 1976[9] gives a different impression.
While he suggests that Milton is one of the people of
fundamental importance for the decade (361), there seems

to be a jaundiced eye cast on the major authors: Milton, like Shakespeare, is one "essentially residual, part of the mind of the time as he is part of ours, available for allusion by anyone on any subject" (355). True though that may be, the impression Golden seems to intend is not cogent. Rather, when the reviewer of Sidney Swinney's *The Battle of Minden, a Poem, in Three Books* in the *Monthly Review* (1769) gives frequent allusions to Milton for this disassociated work, it is because Milton is so readily at the mind's edge as a kind of archetypal poet. Butler and Prior are not called to mind, probably for the simple reason that they were not in the reviewer's dominant consciousness at all. Gratuitous reference to Milton's alleged failure at the sonnet emerges in a review of Hugh Downman's *The Land of the Muses* in the *Critical Review* (1768); the allusions in the *Critical Reviewer*'s remarks on *The Life of Mr. James Quin, Comedian* (1766), or on Thomas Morell's *Thesaurus Græcæ Poeseos* (1762), or on *A New Estimate of Manners and Principles* (1760), or on *The Law of Nations; or Principles of the Law of Nature* (1760), suggest to me that "residual" is hardly the right word.

This is not to say that the average person of the times really knew Milton or read him, any more than we can say that everyone who mentions Mr. Spock has seen one of the Star Trek shows or movies—I for one have not—but it is to say that someone like James Joyce stands for a kind of writing (rightly or wrongly) among those who have a literate background, even though they probably have not read *Finnegans Wake* and never heard of *Exiles*. And we may remind ourselves that for Milton, only some specific works or popular biographical anecdotes get cited. But then not every well-published Miltonists has necessarily read all of Milton, I daresay: *Declaration, or Letters Patents*? *Brief Notes Upon a Late Sermon*? all of *De doctrina christiana*? the psalm translations? It is rather the incidental, casual use of an author in some out-of-the-way place that delineates reputation (if not really knowledge) of an author. I think of John Cleland's quotation from *Areopagitica* in *The Way to Things by Words, and To Words by Things* (1766); of Nathaniel Ames's poem for February in his *Astronomical Diary* for 1765; of the second president of the United States John Adams's discussions of Of *Education* in his diary, under date of February 1763; of the influence on Samuel Johnson of Cheshire's play *The Blazing Comet* (1732); of the misquoted lines from book 12 that serve as a title page epigraph to the anonymous *The Young Senator. A Satyre. With an Epistle to Mr. Fielding, on his Studying the Law* (1738); of Peter Whalley's discussion of Milton's style in his *Essay on the Manner of Writing History* (1746); of James Fortescue's *A View of Life in Its Several Passions. With a Preliminary Discourse on Moral Writing* (1749).

In the two magazines in the 1760s that Golden studies for his essay, we find unexpected references or discussions, such as Milton's teaching languages to his daughters in a notice of *The Method of Calculating an Eclipse Geometrically* by Daniel Fenning and John Probat (*Monthly Review*, 1764) and Adam's language and Milton's principles of composition in a review of Thomas Leland's *A Dissertation on the Principles of Human Eloquence* (*Critical Review*, 1764). Milton does not make Golden's first list of authors with five or more major references, although I am not sure how he could in a review journal of the mid-1700s unless it were reviewing a book or edition devoted to Milton. (In the British Isles there were at least 19 editions of *Paradise Lost*, six of *Paradise Regain'd*, six of the *Poetical Works*, two of the oratorio of *Paradise Lost*, one of John Wesley's extract from *Paradise Lost*, four of the theatrical adaptation of *Comus*, six of Händel's *Samson*, and two of the musical adaptation of "Lycidas," during 1760–1767. There are no editions in 1768–1769.) But there are fairly extensive discussions in such reviews as those on John Christopher Smith's oratorio of *Paradise Lost* (*Monthly Review*, 1760); William Massey's *Remarks upon Milton's "Paradise Lost"* (*Monthly Review*, 1761); Daniel Webb's *Remarks on the Beauties of Poetry* (*Critical Review*, 1762); *Anecdotes of Polite Literature* (*Critical Review*, 1764), which talks about Addison's critique of the epic; John Ogilvie's *Solitude: Or, the Elysium of the Poets, a Vision* (*Critical Review*, 1766), which presents Milton's "garden"; M. Formey's *Elementary Principles of the Belle Lettres* (*Critical Review*, 1766), which discusses Dupré de Saint Maur's translation of *Paradise Lost* and Milton; a French translation of "L'Allegro et Le Pensieroso de Milton, Traduits en Vers françois" (*Monthly Review*, 1766); and William Jackson's *Lycidas: A Musical Entertainment* (*Monthly Review*, 1767). Then, too, there is the application of Edmund Burke's aesthetic principles to Milton's works in the *Monthly Review* (1769) of *A Letter to his Excellency Count * * * on Poetry, Painting, and Sculpture.*

Indeed, four typical reviews in the *Critical Review* in 1761, 1767, and 1769 indicate Milton's presence for the age, a presence that saw him as a criterion of taste, a source of knowledge, and an author to be reckoned with. The review of Allan Ramsay's *The Nuptials. A Didactic Poem* indicates its great indebtedness to Milton; one of William Harris's *An Historical and Critical Account of the Life of Oliver Cromwell* even reprints a quotation from Sonnet 16; and two on Catherine Macaulay (Graham)'s *The History of England from the Accession of James 1 to the Elevation of the House of Hanover* indicate her unacknowledged use of *Eikonoklastes* and, at the same time, disagree (as might be expected) with Milton's view of Charles I, a continuing issue for the age, underlying much antagonism to Milton the man from more than just Samuel Johnson, despite the praise of Milton the poet.

THREE

Milton's Eighteenth Century Influence: Aesthetic Theory

That John Milton was a major influence on eighteenth century literature and religious ideas is a well-known and often repeated belief. James Thorpe noted that "Criticism centered on *Paradise Lost,* which was venerated as a principal support of the orthodox creed" as well as "his 'sublimity'—the capacity of his poetry to enlarge the imagination of the reader."[1] Some people, indeed, seemed to have learned much that was considered biblical from the poem. Earlier in the century, Milton's artistry "was eyed suspiciously"; in midcentury "attention turned to subtle matters of style; and even at the end of the century Milton's artistic purpose in studied variations from the basic pattern of his verse had hardly been examined."[2] There were numerous imitations of the versification of *Paradise Lost* through poems in blank verse (often called "Miltonicks") and of "L'Allegro" and "Il Penseroso" in poems employing octosyllabic couplets; the diction, language, imagery of these three poems and of "A Mask" ("Comus" as the eighteenth century renamed it) constantly reemerged along with appropriations and pointed allusions in the poetry of the century.

Peter Hägin's study of epics during these years advanced the thesis that Milton's masterwork strongly contributed to the decline (even demise) of heroic poetry through the inability of others to emulate it successfully, except perhaps in parodic forms, and through what we nowadays might call an anxiety of influence.[3] A fairly recent book by Dustin Griffin counters the generally alleged deleterious influence of Milton by a more informed and more sympathetic view of eighteenth century poetry. "While, admittedly, second-rate writers seized on superficial or merely technical features of Milton's works, his blank verse prosody or octosyllabic measure, his Latinate diction or his inverted syntax," Griffin explains, "greater writers saw deeper and found inspiration in Milton's great myth of a lost garden of innocence, in his recurrent and related themes of freedom, choice, and responsibility, his celebration of marriage, his defiant stance against his detractors."[4]

However, an area of Milton's importance within the century that remains almost totally undiscussed is his significance for aesthetic theory. In aesthetic theory, the increased understanding of Milton's poetic achievement moved away from the concepts of authority—which had led to mere imitation—and of revelation—advanced earlier by Joseph Addison and John Dennis—to philosophical analysis of the beautiful, an inheritance of the Enlightenment fostered in the decades of the midcentury.

Milton's epic was translated and imitated in England, the American colonies, France, Italy, Germany, Holland, Spain, Portugal, Russia, Poland, Hungary, and Denmark;

the companion poems, "L'Allegro" and "Il Penseroso," furnished prosodic form, subject matter, and contrastive treatments; "Comus," "Lycidas," *Paradise Regain'd*, and *Samson Agonistes* provided a more limited but a definite influence as well. Quotations, partial quotations, and allusions abound in creative works of the period. But as the century proceeded, the intellectual influence of Milton was seen not only in creative works like poetry, the drama, and the novel, but also in educational works like Joseph Priestley's *A Course of Lectures on Oratory and Criticism* (London, 1777),[5] or Claude Helvetius's *A Treatise on Man, His Intellectual Faculties and His Education* (London, 1777),[6] or Robert Lowth's *A Short Introduction to English Grammar: With Critical Notes* (London, 1762);[7] and in political treatises like James Burgh's *Political Disquisitions: or, An Enquiry into Public Errors, Defects, and Abuses* (London, 1774).[8]

For many poets, Milton became the author to be imitated by direct reproduction of form, language, style, and subject matter. The discussion of *Paradise Lost* by Joseph Addison went a long way toward establishing Milton as authority, which was the basic nature of his influence on aesthetic theory at that time. In his first of the *Spectator* papers, no. 267, 5 January 1712, Addison examined the qualifications of an epic poem and found Milton's work superior even to the ancients: first in the fable, second the action, third its greatness. And Milton "has filled his Story with so many surprising Incidents, which bear so close Analogy with what is delivered in Holy Writ, that it is capable of pleasing the most delicate Reader, without giving Offence to the most scrupulous." It was this authority and its imitative detritis that Jonathan Swift, while praising Milton and the style of his epic, warned against in his *Letter of Advice to a Young Poet: Together with a Proposal for the Encouragement of Poetry in this Kingdom*

(Dublin, 1721). Milton's authority, indeed, became so great that in midcentury William Lauder contrived a scheme to reduce his position by alleging plagiarism through manufactured "sources." And while he too was greatly influenced by Milton, William Wordsworth at the end of the century pilloried the poetasters preceding who were mere imitators of language and style.

Early on, Milton was also praised for his presentation of religion in revelatory terms in *Paradise Lost. In The Grounds of Criticism in Poetry* (1704), John Dennis gives us nine "rules for employing religion in poetry," all of which are exemplified in Milton, but for Dennis, others like Edmund Spenser and Abraham Cowley "miscarried" in one or more. For example, "Religion ought to be one, that the Poet may be mov'd by it, and . . . he may appear to be in earnest" (1); "Religion may be managed so as to promote the Violence of the Enthusiastick Passions, and their Change and Variety" (4); "the divine and human Persons, if there be any, may have Inclinations and Affections" but "they be fairly distinguish'd from the human Persona by the same Inclinations and Affections" (7, 9). Dennis continues:

> I know several gentlemen of very good Sense, who are extremely mov'd by Milton's Hymn, in the fifth Book of *Paradise Lost*, and hardly at all stir'd with the Translation of the 148th Psalm, from whence that Hymn is taken. . . . we may conclude, that the Passion or Enthusiasm in that Hymn is exactly in Nature; that is, that the Enthusiasm, or Passion, or Spirit, call it what you will, flows from the Ideas, and bears a just Proportion to them.

Such revelatory abilities of Milton's poem may be seen in Benjamin Colman's second sermon published in *A Discourse on the Incomprehensibleness of God: In Four Sermons, Preached at the Lecture in Boston, A. D. 1714.*

Colman paraphrases ideas in *Paradise Lost* to make a point of the great prescience of God.[9]

Perhaps we should note as well Milton's continued importance in the matter of divorce, as in Matthew George Schroeder's "De Misogynia Erditorvm, von Abelgesinnten Gelehrten gegen das weibliche Geschichte" (1717), where Milton's arguments are advanced anew as remedy for a man's difficulties with a wife; or Godfrey Boettner's "De Malis Eruditorum Uxoribus (Vulgo) Von den bosen Weibern der Gelehrten" (1705), which argues expectations of conjugal compatibility straight out of Milton.[10]

As the century wears on, however, the focus moves from authority to example, from the revelatory to the rational, and we can see this in such analyses as Edmund Burke's in *A Philosophical Enquiry into the Origin of Our Ideas of the Sublime and Beautiful* (1756). "The ideas of eternity, and infinity, are among the most affecting we have," he writes. In sublime descriptions of eternity,

> The mind is hurried out of itself, by a croud of great and confused images; which affect because they are crouded and confused. For separate them, and you lose much of the greatness, and join them, and you infallibly lose the clearness. The images raised by poetry are always of this obscure kind; though in general the effects of poetry, are by no means to be attributed to the images it raises.

His example for his remarks is Milton's portrait of Satan in 1.589–99:

> Whoever attentively considers this passage of Milton, and indeed all of the best and most affecting descriptions of poetry, will find, that it does not in general produce its end by raising the images of things, but by exciting a passion similar to that which real objects excite by other instruments.[11]

For James Burnet, Lord Monbaddo, in *Of the Origin and Progress of Language*, speaking of passages and lines from *Paradise Lost*, says:

> This kind of plain work is entirely out of fashion in our poetry, . . . and but little used even in our prose, and every thing in both is embroidery and ornament. But the taste of Milton, and I may add of the age in which he wrote, was very different; for in him we have many passages, not only beautiful, but even sublime, without metaphor or figure, or any thing of what is now called *fine language.* [12]

For James Beattie, the aesthetic ideal lay in "A richer vein of invention, as well as a more correct taste," something observed in Milton but not in his mere imitators.

> The style of his numbers has not often been imitated with success. It is not merely the want of rhyme, nor the diversified position of pauses, nor the drawing out of the sense from one line to another; far less is it the mixture of antiquated words and strange idioms, that constitutes the charm of Milton's versification; though many of his imitators, when they copy him in these or in some of these respects, think they have acquitted themselves very well."
> (*Essays*, "On the Utility of Classical Learning," 1776) [13]

These attributes will not lead to the re-creation of beauty: beauty is not achieved by imitation. Nor is the work they sustain the kind of manifestation that reveals in its analysis the means to re-create beauty. Rather, *Paradise Lost* is example, an example that works upon one's passions: it does not serve as an agent, and it is a manifestation of itself, not of some other.

Example and the rational underlie Hugh Blair's analysis of the sublime. Speaking of the description of Satan in book 1 as head of the infernal host, Blair writes (1759):

> Here concur a variety of sources of the sublime: the principal object eminently great; a high superior nature,

fallen indeed, but erecting itself against distress, the grandeur of the principal object heightened, by associating it with so noble an idea as that of the sun suffering an eclipse; this picture shaded with all those images of change and trouble, of darkness and terror, which coincide so finely with the Sublime emotion; and the whole expressed in a style and versification, easy, natural, and simple, but magnificent.[14]

"The Author appears, upon some occasions, a Metaphysician and a Divine, rather than a Poet. But the general tenor of his work is interesting; he seizes and fixes the imagination; engages, elevates, and affects us as we proceed . . . ," Blair continues. Like others from Dryden onward who succumbed to a preconception of "correctness," Blair finds lapses in *Paradise Lost*, and he would probably have conceded George, Lord Lyttelton's remark that "The bright and excessive blaze of poetical fire, which shines in so many parts of the *Paradise Lost*, will hardly permit the dazzled eye to see its faults."[15] Yet Blair's concepts of sublimity in objects and in writing, of personification, comparison, harmony, the oppositions of simplicity and affectation of style, are drawn often from the poem as he reads it. This problem of "correctness" begins to disappear as the Romantic age approaches, but as Thorpe indicated, no general understanding of Milton's artistry and studied variations had been achieved despite the example the epic had become.

Forty years later (1798) William Thomson in *An Enquiry into the Elementary Principles of Beauty, in the Works of Nature and Art. To which is prefixed, An Introductory Discourse of Taste* specifically rejects the textual revisions of Richard Bentley in discussing the sublimity of *Paradise Lost* 3.21–24. He is not concerned with "correctness"; rather, *Paradise Lost* furnishes examples of what is sublime. This is Monbaddo's approach as well: "This author I have Frequently mentioned before," he notes, "and shall, in the sequel, quote him oftener than any other English writer, because I consider him as the best standard for style, and all the ornaments of speech, that we have in our language."

Thomson also cites Milton often in talking of beauty in nature. In a way this harks back to Stephen Switzer's employment of the garden in his descriptions of rural landscapes, gardening, and trees in *The Nobleman, Gentleman, and Gardener's Recreation: or, An Introduction to Gardening, Planting, Agriculture, and the Other Business and Pleasures of a Country Life* (1715). The differences are the differences of the movement in time within the century: Switzer is enthusiastic and exalted by Milton's words and sees them as description of what the gardener should achieve; Thomson looks at nature and reminds his reader that Milton had so described it.

The anonymous author of the section on the senses in the *Encyclopédie* says, in words apparently drawn from Father Buffier's *Traité des Premières Verités*, that

> Our philosophers only seem to take into account that pleasure of feeling which accompanies simple ideas of sensation. But there exist a great many agreeable feelings within those complex notions of objects which we call "beautiful" or "harmonious." It does not matter whether or not such notions of beauty and harmony are called "external sense perceptions" of sight and hearing. They should really be called an "internal sense" or an "internal feeling" if only to distinguish them from those other sensations of sight or hearing which can exist without any perception of beauty or harmony.

Francis Hutcheson, 30 years earlier in *An Inquiry into the Original of Our Ideas of Beauty and Virtue*, spoke of our approbation of or delight in external objects in a section concerning the power of custom in relation to internal senses, and contended a like position:

had we no *natural* Sense of *Beauty* from *Uniformity*, *Custom* could never have made us image any *Beauty* in Objects; if we had had no *Ear*, *Custom* could never have given us the Pleasures of *Harmony*. When we have these natural *Senses* antecedently, *Custom* may make us capable of extending our Views further, and of receiving more complex Ideas of *Beauty* in Bodys, or *Harmony in Sounds*, by increasing our Attention and quickness of Perception. But however *Custom* may increase our Power of receiving or comparing complex Ideas, yet it seems rather to weaken than strengthen the Ideas of *Beauty*, or the Impressions of Pleasure from regular Objects; else how is it possible that any Person could go into the open Air on a sunny Day, or clear Evening, without the most extravagant Raptures, such as Milton represents our *Ancestor* in upon his first Creation? For such any Person would certainly fall into, upon the first Representation of such a Scene (p. 89, 1726 Second Edition)

Hutcheson has called upon Milton, as he does elsewhere, to sustain the aesthetic point being made. Milton provides example (and though other authors do, too, he is one of the most prominent and most repeated by various writers); Milton's work, especially *Paradise Lost*, offers rational recognition of a truth, an underlying philosophic proposition.

This question of external and internal senses lies beneath Henry Home, Lord Kames's view about elevated objects and their relationship with the sublime. In chapter 4 on Grandeur and Sublimity in *The Elements of Criticism* (1762), he acknowledges that "The qualities of grandeur and beauty are not more distinct, than the emotions are which these qualities produce in a spectator . . . [It is] evident, that grandeur is satisfied with a less degree of regularity . . . than is requisite for beauty." A beautiful object placed high appears more agreeable and produces in the spectator what he calls "the emotion of sublimity."

While quotations from other authors are given, it is a much longer quotation of *PL* 4.131–49 that "is a fine illustration of the impression made by elevated objects." Then talking of height and lowness, he adds, "And in this may visibly be discovered peculiar attention in fitting the internal constitution of man to his external circumstances."

Further, of dissimilar emotions and passions, Kames remarks, "In reading the description of the dismal waste, book 1 of *Paradise Lost,* we are sensible of a confused feeling, arising from dissimilar emotions forc'd into union, to wit, the beauty of the description, and the horror of the object described [and he quotes 1.180–83]. And with respect to this and many similar passages in *Paradise Lost,* we are sensible, that the emotions being obscured by each other, make neither of them that figure they would make separately." Of gardening and architecture, he writes:

> Regularity is required in that part of a garden which is adjacent to the dwelling-house; because an immediate accessory ought to partake the regularity of the principal object: but in proportion to the distance from the house considered as the centre, regularity ought less and less to be studied; for in an extensive plan, it hath a fine effect to lead the mind insensibly from regularity to a bold variety.

And of course, it is Milton who supplies a fit example of the theory, implying that Milton, creative artist, was aware of this proposition well before its formulation here: "Milton, describing the garden of Eden, prefers justly grandeur before regularity:

> Flowrs worthy of Paradise which not nice Art
> In Beds and curious Knots, but Nature boon
> Powrd forth profuse on Hill and Dale and Plain,
> The open field, and where the unpierc't shade
> Imbrownd the noontide Bowrs."

Kames analyzes aesthetic aspects of writing rather than purely philosophic concepts, and it is repeatedly Milton's work that is cited, along with other authors', when he writes of the beauty of language, versification, comparisons, figures, personifications, epic and dramatic compositions, and the like. Under "Description," for example, we find: "In the following passage, the action, with all its material circumstances, is represented so much to the life, that it would scarce appear more distinct to a real spectator; and it is the manner of description that contributes greatly to the sublimity of the passage." He quotes *PL* 1.663–69.

The aesthetics developed in the latter part of the century are influenced by the work of Milton and yet can be seen to argue against the reflection of Milton's influence in many of the authors of the immediate past. What occurs is a move from model to mentor in the shape of Milton, from classifying his work as a rather simple description of what exists in nature (and religion) to viewing it as a window into an analysis of nature, which can be contemplated and understood only from many angles of vision. Two examples must suffice to complete this essay, which could be amplified by numerous other authors and other works.

James Beattie in "An Essay on Poetry and Music, As They Affect the Mind," chapter 1, section 3, writes:

> When Michael, in the eleventh book of *Paradise Lost*, announces to Adam and Eve the necessity of their immediate departure from the garden of Eden, the poet's art in preserving the decorum of the two characters is very remarkable. Pierced to the heart at the thought of leaving that happy place, Eve, in all the violence of ungovernable sorrow, breaks forth into a pathetic apostrophe to Paradise, to the flowers she had reared, and to the nuptial bower she had adorned. Adam makes no address to the walks, the trees, or the flowers of the garden, the loss whereof did not

so much afflict him; but, in his reply to the Archangel, expresses, without a figure, his regret for being banished from a place where he had so oft been honoured with a sensible manifestation of the Divine Presence. The use of apostrophe in the one case, and the omission of it in the other, not only gives a beautiful variety to the style, but also marks that superior elevation and composure of mind, by which the poet had all along distinguished the character of Adam.— One of the finest applications of this figure that is any where to be seen, in the fourth book of the same Poem; where the author, catching by sympathy the devotion of our first parents, suddenly drops his narrative, and joins his voice to theirs in adoring the Father of the universe. [*PL* 4.720-27]. Milton took the hint of this fine contrivance from a well-known passage of Virgil: . . . . The beauty arising from diversified composition is the same in both, and very great in each. But every reader must feel, that the figure is incomparably more affecting to the mind in the imitation, than in the original. So true it is, that the most rational emotions raise the most intense fellow-feeling; and that the apostrophe is then the most emphatical, when it displays those workings of human affection, which are at once ardent, and well founded.

The second example of this move to seeing Milton as mentor is Uvedale Price's insistence in *Essay on the Picturesque, as Compared with the Sublime and the Beautiful* (1796) that "The limbs of huge trees shattered by lightning or temptuous winds, are in the highest degree picturesque; but whatever is caused by those dreaded powers of destruction, must always have a tincture of the sublime." And noting a pertinent simile in Ariosto, he remarks: "Milton seems to have thought of this simile; but the sublimity both of his subject and of his own genius, made him reject those picturesque circumstances, the variety of which, while it amuses, distracts the mind, and has kept it fixed on a few grand and awful images: [*PL* 1.612–15]." Milton is cited and quoted often throughout Price's valuable discussions. One of the longer ones follows:

> A blaze of light unmixed with shade, on the same principles tends to the sublime only: Milton has placed light in its most glorious brightness, as an inaccessible barrier round the throne of the Almighty: [*PL* 3.3–51]. And such is the power he has given even to its diminished splendor, [3.381–82]. In one place, indeed, he has introduced very picturesque circumstances in his sublime representation of the deity: but it is of the deity in wrath; it is when from the weakness and narrowness of our conceptions, we give the names and the effects of our passions, to the all-perfect Creator: [6.56–59]. In general, however, where the glory, power, or majesty of God are represented, he has avoided that variety of form and colouring, which might take off from simple and uniform grandeur; and has encompassed the divine essence with unapproached light, or with the majesty of darkness.

In aesthetic theory, the increased understanding of Milton's poetic achievement emboldened the philosophic analysis of the beautiful: it became a window into the analysis of nature.

FOUR

Miltonesque: Triumphs and Failures in Eighteenth Century Poetry

S tudents of eighteenth century and early Romantic poetry can become easily confused when asked to trace Milton's influence on those periods. They may know that *Paradise Lost*, "Comus," "L'Allegro," and "Il Penseroso" were popular and imitated or adapted throughout the 1700s, but they also may recall that Wordsworth objected to "deluges of idle and extravagant stories in verse," the popularity of which he laid to the neglect of such works as Milton's. Further, Wordsworth impaled much poetry that clearly emerged from the Miltonic tradition because that poetry lacked incidents and situations from common life, it lacked language really used by human beings, its action and situation gave importance to the feeling rather than the other way around, its abstract ideas were personified as a mechanical device of style, and such poetry abounded in "poetic diction."

Yet Milton, to whose influence these poetic criticisms can be traced—though not exclusively, of course—was well beloved by the Romantics and was a major influence upon them. Wordsworth wrote, "Poetry is the image of man and nature," and thereby implied that the eighteenth century poetry to which he was reacting presented something else: rationality rather than emotion, mechanistic devices and techniques rather than passionate truth. Another way of expressing it is the difference between the spontaneous overflow of powerful feelings professed by Wordsworth and an apparent emphasis on genre, form, and taste, assigned to his immediate predecessors.[1] The seeming confusion in these supposedly mutually exclusive views is dissolved by an awareness of the nature of eighteenth century imitation, by an understanding of the influence upon the Romantics and by a less superficial knowledge of what eighteenth century poetry is. But it is curious that a Wordsworth could not see any better beneath the surface in his time than could an Irving Babbitt in his maltreatment of the Romantics in the twentieth century.

This is not to say that all eighteenth century or Romantic poetry is successful or commendable to all tastes, but it is to suggest that more is going on in the poetry of these periods than has generally been acknowledged, although recent studies have gone a long way in correcting the generalities of literary handbooks. One way of attacking this problem of conflicts is by examination of the Janus-influence of Milton on eighteenth century poetry, and thus my aim here is to describe two movements enhanced by the authority of Milton, which oppose each other in direction and rationale. One movement will be seen a completion (if any movement is ever completed) of a trend begun in or at least by the sixteenth century; the other will evidence the persistence and growth of a contrary direction and rationale, which flowers in the Romantic age.[2] The last century and a quarter since the sixteenth century can be viewed as a vacillation between these opposing movements, the more dominant at any period being governed as much by reaction to the immediate past as any ideological crisis one wants to erect as reason.

These movements describe a paradox that hangs over the thought and literature of the Renaissance and the post-Renaissance: that which helped move western Europe out of the medieval world became the ideational source for neoclassicism, but in turn neoclassicism evoked Romantic reactions which in certain ways, came to equate a return to pre-Renaissance attitudes. I refer to the philosophic change that saw a systematization of such areas of thought as logic, religion, government, science, and literature.[3] The "modernism" that the closure systems of the sixteenth century predicated—and indeed still do predicate for some—fostered in literature sets of rules, based upon unflinching definitions and such interpretations of earlier critics as Castelvetro's version of Aristotle's dramatic observations. While great creative artists like Shakespeare could lampoon this reductive tendency in Polonius's talk of "The best actors in the world, either for tragedy, comedy, history, pastoral, pastoral-comical, historical-pastoral, tragical-historical, tragical-comical-historical-pastoral, scene individable, or poem unlimited," lesser authors wrote to formula and adopted Roger Ascham's principle of imitation of other writers rather than mimesis of nature.[4] And nature itself was being formulized, to culminate in the scientific achievements of the eighteenth century, a process that has generally been only extended, not advanced, in the last two centuries.

The aesthetics of the past had allowed an author's free spirit to control that which it observed in literature and to dare to be different, but Renaissance aesthetics had increasingly become characterized by an author's taking over of form and language and subject and treatment from others. The question over the authorship of the love elegy "The Expostulation" is merely a case in point: for it has seemed to many to be John Donne's, to others to be Ben Jonson's, and yet to others to be Sir John Roe's. Much as we like to think Donne's and Jonson's styles to be distinct unto themselves (and certainly different from each other's), there are elements in some of their poems which are so undistinctive that questions like authorship can arise. That, of course, is the main problem with assigning "Hobson's Epitaph" to Milton with any surety as well: neither it nor the two acknowledged Hobson poems show elements that are distinctively Miltonic, and all three draw elements (language, wit, puns, ideas, form) from a myriad of other verses on the carrier. These kinds of poems—the love elegies or the witty Hobson exercises— are examples of the competitive spirit of poetic writing during the Renaissance; they do much to deny personal involvement, elements, ideas, and attitudes within such work. What becomes increasingly obvious as the Renaissance proceeds and declines, and the Restoration emerges and melds into the eighteenth century, is that a poet's "signature" (Leslie Fiedler's term) tends to disappear except for those of true poetic worth, and then only in such poetic work that dares to be different.

While we may call the kind of aesthetic theory coming to the fore in the Renaissance "the doctrine of imitation" or "neoclassicism," it is a poetic that emphasized structure and form rather than ornament (and thus stressed certain genres while ignoring others[5]), a poetic that revelled in impersonality, a poetic that was didactic (employing the concept of *dulce et utile* with a vengeance), a poetic of conformity. There was a "correct" way and an "incorrect" way of writing that involved subject matter, genre, decorum, language, prosody, and style. Everyone seems to know that Samuel Johnson found no "effusion of real passion" in "Lycidas" because "passion runs not after remote allusions and obscure opinions"; that it was "disgusting" because "its form is that of pastoral"; that the sonnets "deserve not any particular criticism" since "the fabrick of a sonnet, however adapted to the Italian language has never succeeded in ours, which, having greater variety of termination, requires the rhymes to be often changed."[6] But the most grievous fault in "Lycidas" is that "With these trifling fictions are mingled the most awful and sacred truths, such as ought never to be polluted with such irreverend combinations." Such aberration of decorum, in the eighteenth century sense, and the other faults that Johnson sees in Milton are clearly a result of the fact that his poems do not fit predetermined molds, the "rules."

But Johnson is only typical of the age.[7] George Lyttelton in a letter to his father, dated 4 February 1728, remarks that poetical license "is no reason why good authors may not raise and animate their works with flights and sallies of imagination, provided they are cautious of restraining them within the bonds of justness and propriety; for nothing can license a poet to offend against Truth and Reason, which are as much the rules of the sublime as less exalted poetry . . . . The sixth book [of *Paradise Lost*] is, I fear, in many places, an exception to this rule; the *poetica licentia* is stretched too far, and *the just is* sacrificed to *the wonderful*. . . ."[8] Lewis Theobald's view of Richard Bentley's emendations of *Paradise Lost* offers an exact example of the kind of attitude we are dealing with in the eighteenth century: "the chief turn of his Criticism is plainly to shew the World, that if *Milton* did not write as He would have him, he ought to have wrote so."[9] And for many, particularly in the Restoration and earlier eighteenth century, Milton's blank verse was a horror, as it was generally for Johnson, too. As noted elsewhere, Thomas Rymer's unfulfilled promise in *The Tragedies of the Last Age* (1678) to "assert *Rime* against the slender Sophistry wherewith [Milton] attacques it" raises a major criticism that reechoes during these years, as in John Clarke's comment:

> Besides these Faults in the Plan of *Paradise Lost*, there is another observable in that admired Poem, viz. the Negligence of the Author with respect to the smoothness of his Verse, which is sometimes scarce distinguishable from Prose. . . . If a Man pretends to write Verse, let it be Verse indeed, and not move on here and there with a Roughness scarce allowable in Prose.[10]

Another way of expressing the development of attitude toward Milton in the eighteenth century is that which operates as an underlying thesis of a collection of essays entitled *Milton and the Line of Vision*.[11] While most attention has been paid to an "Aristotelian" principle of imitation that develops the line of wit, methodizing but praising variation as well, an unstinted undercurrent of "Platonic" "truth" persists to establish a line of vision. The "Platonic" poet becomes a copyist (a quite different concept from that of being an imitator) of the poet's own vision. The employment of the Bible is a clear demarcation between these antithetic poets, the one reproducing, for example, event or character, the other interpreting the revelation in the event or character. Such revelation becomes archetypal and is fundamental to prophecy, an act of little interest to a Pope or a Johnson.[12]

For the most part, eighteenth century poetry came out of a seventeenth century concerned with an interpretation of Horace's "ut pictura poesis." Poetry offered a reflection of the real world, a "speaking picture," and the basis of evaluation is therefore clearly the closeness to the pictures of this world. One "imitated" these pictures. In a sense, this poetry dealt with the external lineaments of things, and one depicted this speaking picture for the inner fancy of the reader. Wit, following Hobbes, was the assemblage of ideas put together with celerity—an "idea" represented by many different kinds of "pictures," thereby defined by numerous analogic materials. Wit implied quickness and variety and strong resemblances. The pictures that wit transmitted to the fancy were to be agreeable "visions," and the difference within the opposite poetic movement we are talking about is the difference in the meaning of the word "fancy."[13] "Vision" for the poet of the line of wit was the composite picture resultant in the reader's fancy from the numerous pictures of the poem.[14]

"Vision" for the Romantics and their older cousins involved prophecy and interpretation: the prophecy took the reader into the realm of future action and belief, with an accompanying sense of the ideal, and the interpretation demanded that the reader see the poem in terms beyond the realities that gave the poem substance. One might expect the poem within the line of wit to present "incidents and situations from common life" in real language, but paradoxically the pictures became more and more unassociated with the world of humankind and more and more imitated from those who had gone before; that is, they became reflections of actuality only. And one might expect the poem within the line of vision to lose association with the observable reality around one, but paradoxically the pictures were more and more a copying of nature in order to impress upon the reader the commonalty of life experience throughout time, thus leading to a mythopoeic realization that within the present is the past, which, fully understood, will bring humankind to new heights and ideals.

The line of wit clearly played upon controls and artifice;

the poem was more cerebration than emotion. Imagery was to be linked as revelatory of the poet and the poet's emotions; perceiving such linkage, the reader would simulate associated thoughts. The poet employed rhetorical and structural parallelism, therefore, to emphasize such linkage, and antithesis to underscore it. If genre, particularly as used and developed by a predecessor, implied certain contexts or attitudes, the poet worked within that genre in order to raise such contexts or attitudes for the poet's own work as well. Some variation was possible, but not much. It is clear that the poet and the poet's "signature" would disappear as the generalization of concepts came to dominate the work. The poetry became more artificial in the sense that Joyce talked of becoming the artificer of his race (in *A Portrait of the Artist as a Young Man*) and in the sense that Ben Jonson spoke of the poet as maker.

The poets of the eighteenth century who followed this line of creativity strove very consciously for specific effects, and any judgment upon their results must evaluate their discernment of ideas and their "wittiness" in the specifically Hobbesian sense. One should not condemn such an approach to writing, as has been fairly common in recent years for eighteenth century poetry, though it has not extended to twentieth century practitioners, simply because an opposing approach is more to someone's ideological or emotional liking. The poetry of the eighteenth century most frequently thought of as epitomizing that century results from a closure movement, as suggested before. The poetic duplication of the past within set parameters (of genre, prosody, decorum, etc.), employing most specifically Ramistic categorization by parallels and antitheses and by constant subdivision, puts the line of wit into a broader movement of culture than has generally been assigned.

Perhaps the reasons for the seemingly sharp turn of

events in poetic as we approach the nineteenth century include a feeling of increased mechanization of all aspects of life, with an accompanying decline in the value of the individual; a sense of being "locked in" to positions in life; a kind of fleshlessness and mere rote action developed within the realm of poetry; and surely the dreary poetry that imitation sometimes produced. Demonstrated may be the way in which some authors of the eighteenth century viewed "any occasion as a 'scene' or a stage for dramatizing the self as a performer." Their "participation would be measured by powers of rendition rather than by efforts of understanding."[15] But some of the poetry was decidedly not dreary, and some of the "romantic" attitude can be observed in other poetry and criticism of the age. Let us look at some of the "minor" poetry of the period, some of which is successful and some of which, for many people, is probably not.

William Collins's 12 odes, published in 1746 as *Odes On Several Descriptive and Allegoric Subjects* (dated 1747), observe one side of the Miltonic influence in the category of "the doctrine of imitation." In addition to the Pindaric Latin ode to John Rouse, with its deliberate variations in prosody and treatment, Milton's "odes" were and are usually considered to include "On the Morning of *Christs* Nativity" (the so-called "Nativity Ode") and "On Time," "Upon the Circumcision," and "At a Solemn Music" (the "English odes"). For the eighteenth century such a classical odist as Horace was a major influence, and the odic tradition in England had been advanced by Ben Jonson and Abraham Cowley. But Milton also was important, and in Collins's 1747 volume Milton was cited in the fourth poem, "Ode on the Poetical Character," pp. 17–18, with echoes of *Paradise Lost*, books 2 and 4 coming immediately to mind:

High on some Cliff, to Heav'n up-pil'd,
Of rude Access, of Prospect wild,
Where, tangled round the jealous Steep,
Strange Shades o'erbrow the Valleys deep,
And holy *Genii* guard the Rock,
Its Gloomes embrown, its Springs unlock,
While on its rich ambitious Head,
And *Eden*, like his own, lies spread.
I view that Oak, the fancied Glades among,
By which as Milton lay, His Ev'ning Ear,
From many a Cloud that drop'd Ethereal Dew,
Nigh spher'd in Heav'n its native Strains could hear:
On which that ancient Trump he reach'd was hung
   Thither oft his Glory greeting,
   From *Waller's* Myrtle Shades retreating,
With many a Vow from Hope's aspiring Tongue,
My trembling Feet his guiding Steps pursue;
   In vain—Such Bliss to One alone,
   Of all the Sons of Soul was known,
   And Heav'n, and *Fancy*, kindred Pow'rs,
   Have now o 'erturn'd th' inspiring Bow'rs,
Or curtain'd close such Scene from ev'ry future View.

Clearly this third section of the ode (a kind antistrophe[16]) has remembered *Paradise Lost* in language and "pictures" (as well as "Arcades," 61–73), and the greatness of the epic has "curtain'd close such Scene from ev'ry future View" (the main thesis of Peter Hägin's study of the decline of epic in the eighteenth century[17]). The remembrance of Satan in Pandemonium at the beginning of book 2 curiously also emerges here for Milton in a poetical Heaven. And the scene is borrowed from Milton's description of Eden, expressed in such Miltonic diction as "Prospect wild," "o'erbrow," "embrown," "His Ev'ning Ear," and "Trump," among other echoes (cf. Sherwin 26 ff.).

75

In the poem, as Sherwin argues, "Collins is delimiting two major categories of eighteenth century aesthetic theory, the Beautiful and Sublime modes" (17), seeing Edmund Spenser as representative of the former and Milton of the latter.[18] While Collins engages genre, form, and taste in his imitation of the language, poetic diction, and action of Spenser's and Milton's poetry, he is far from mechanistic, surely depicting what he and Wordsworth would consider "passionate truth," retreating from the myrtle shades describing—for some at least—Edmund Waller's work. The genre and form are altered rather than slavishly imitated, and what emerges is a strophe moving from one aesthetic to another (to a line of vision); an epode (or mesode), apostrophizing poetry and its powers; and an antistrophe in which poetic hopes are dashed because the height has been reached, and all else is imitation. But in his "imitation," Collins has emulated that height, at the same time that he analyzes and epitomizes what midcentury poetry represents.

Further, the prosody epitomizing the poetical character is both the "same" and different. The strophe and antistrophe are built on iambic tetrameter couplets (1–8), which then become 14 lines of mixed verse, ending with a typically Spenserian hexameter (as Milton did in the "Nativity Ode" stanzas and in "At a Solemn Music"): *a10 b10 c10 b10 a10 d8(9) d8(9) d10 c10 e8 e8 f8 f8 c12.* The epode is in tetrameter couplets only. In other words, the poem's poetic sections are planned, organized, comparative and contrastive of prosody and, at the same time, of subject and treatment. The poem becomes a statement and a demonstration. It is concerned with line of vision, and it engages the line of vision.

Sherwin doubts that Collins knew what he wished to express in "The Manners. An Ode, "41–45; he writes: "What happens when Collins attempts to retrace Milton's path to freedom?—'The Manners,' a poem in which Milton's magic is dissipated at Collins's every touch" (45). Himself a victim of what he charges to Collins, Sherwin chalks up the "disaster" of the poem to Collins's "cultural anxiety and the anxiety of Milton's influence" (68), seeing "an evasion of the parental" source which had been freed from the past in "L'Allegro" and also "an embrace of the ancestral source [medieval romance]." He epitomizes what Milton's influence in eighteenth century poetry was: "more than any other single figure, with the possible exception of Pope, he is responsible for the emergence of a generation of fine sensibilities more prone to admiration than to creation, given more to brooding upon the relationship between reason and imagination than to integrating them" (81). (Reference is also made here to Thomas Gray and James Thomson.) But while this epitome may offer some analytic truth, it also pinpoints a critical attitude that has not given eighteenth century poetic "creation" its due or acknowledged what "imagination" there may be in such a poem as "The Manners."

The problem, I believe, starts with the reading of Milton's work itself. The companion poems have been, and still too often are, read as two versions of Milton's self, two versions of his "ideal" days, two versions of "a ritual of self-purgation" (45) whereby poetic integrity is sought. Had the author of these poems (perhaps written in 1631, while the author was a ministerial student seeking a master's degree) not proceeded to become a poet whose creative productions included *Paradise Lost*, critics might have seen the poems as coterie contributions, reacting to and expanding upon such imitated sources as John Fletcher in "Nice Valour" and Robert Burton in *Anatomy of Melancholy* and, along with Sir Walter Ralegh and John Donne, Christopher Marlowe in "The Passionate Shepherd to His Love." The parallelisms of the two poems should, at least, direct the reader to understand that they do not represent any kind of ritual of self-purgation, much as they may reflect the author's real world or imaginative world.

But if we read them with such a biographical and "sincere" fountainhead, we miss the fun of seeing another view of Marlowe/Ralegh/Donne's seduction theme. In "L'Allegro" the "love" becomes an abstraction, Mirth; in "Il Penseroso," an abstraction, Melancholy. In each poem the possible "gifts" that can persuade the poetic voice to live with each respective "love" are recounted, balancing one set of gifts against another. The poems depict personalities that may be drawn to one or the other love because of the gifts offered (and like most, if not all, people, Milton encompasses both personalities at different times). He is having poetic fun, and he is engaging himself in the act of writing for the sake of the act of writing. If we can see Collins's "The Manners" as another contribution to this *jeu d'esprit*, thus paying attention to the writer writing, we may come to recognize what is creative rather than mere imitation in the poem, what is integrated between reason and imagination.

The poem is in octosyllabic couplets with numerous appropriations from Milton's poems (not only from the companion poems). In the first verse paragraph, the poet says farewell to such matter as informs "L'Allegro" (its first ten lines, of course, had dismissed "Melancholy"); in the second, to such matters as "Il Penseroso" had offered (its first ten lines had dispelled "vain deluding joyes"). The third and fourth verse paragraphs call on a combination of the worlds of "Il Penseroso" and "L'Allegro" through "Science" of Man, that is, Manners. And "young-eyed healthful *Wit*" is called upon "no Delights from Thee [to] divide." "Wit," from the Germanic meaning "to know," emphasizes knowledge and the celerity of its use in Hobbesian terms, not in the modern delimited meaning of "pun." In the next verse paragraph, the poet leaves behind the past, as seen in its fabulous romances, and finally he invokes "Nature," that is, Man in "Each forceful Thought, each prompted Deed," since Nature, the social science of humankind, provides a "Scene-full World." Collins's contribution to this thematic "subgenre" rejects the tinsel of Marlowe's seduction, the cynicism of Ralegh's reaction, and the reversals of Donne's wittiness, and combines the abstractions of Milton's "Sports," for all those delights that can be served up by "Manners" are worthy of pursuit. What is rejected in the poem is the retreat into the "dream" of Art's "enchanted School"; what is accepted is reading Man's native Heart (1. 26). The Band he asks to be admitted to is Humour's (1. 52), and we see in this 78-line poem an interesting balanced construction: lines 1–26, 27–52, 53–78.

For some readers Collins's poem may not be significant or enjoyable; it may not be a "triumph." But it isn't a "failure," either, if one reads the poem itself in its intentionality as a varied view of the thematic "subgenre," if one does not misread Milton and expect a writer influenced by him to overgo him in certain ways—if one takes the poem in its own right. There has been a combination of reason and imagination in the poem, the poet arguing for such a combination but for a rejection of fancy (as the eighteenth century had come to differentiate those terms), and it is a "creation" structured to balance and contrast its parts and its focal points. It may not be what all modern-day readers credit, but that may reflect their attitudes more than the essence of the work itself. It is poetry of wit, if not of vision.

A midcentury author who seems to have few champions is William Mason, a devoted Miltonian in prose, drama, and poetry. In his hands the ode and the pastoral elegy flourished, though not to high praise from the Romantics or later critics. Ode IX, for example, subtitled "To the Naval Officers of Great-Britain. February 11, 1779," on the trial of Admiral Augustus Keppel (later Viscount Keppel), consists of two Pindaric sets of strophe, anti-strophe, and epode. Like Edmund Burke, Mason looked on Keppel as one of the greatest and best men of his age, and so employs a generic form that specifically praises accomplishment for a nation. Keppel was acquitted, but the irony of the charge and the praise is underscored in the first strophe by Mason's use of the allegory of Sin and Death and contrast of godly action:

> Hence to thy Hell! thou fiend accurst,
>   Of Sin's incestuous brood, the worst
>   Whom to pale Death the spectre bore:
>   Detraction hence! 'tis Truth's command;
>   She launches, from her seraph hand,
> The shaft that strikes thee to th'infernal shore.
>   Old England's genius leads her on
>   To vindicate his darling son,
>   Whose fair and veteran fame
>   Thy venom'd tongue had dar'd defile:
>   The goddess comes, and all the isle
> Feels the warm influence of her heav'nly flame.

The reader is not simply to recognize the allegory of Sin and Death from book 2 of *Paradise Lost*, and its extension to their offspring Detraction, whose tongue is appropriately "venom'd." The reader should also see the way in which Truth, as angelic goddess, has been able to vindicate Keppel, just as Milton's Eternal Providence has hoped "to vindicate the ways of God to men." The shaft of Truth reminds the reader of Ithuriel's spear, which, touching the "disguised" Satan, reveals his true identity.

The allusion and appropriations make the issue, for the reader, into more than just an author taking sides in a court

martial case. It propels the reader into the struggle between falsehood and truth, into the opposed forces of
France and England, and into the evils of any war. The
ending of the poem evokes Milton's charge "what can
Warrs but endless warr still breed":

> So shall his own bold auspices prevail,
> Nor fraud's insidious wiles, nor envy pale
> Arrest the force of his victorious band;
> The Gaul subdued, fraternal strife shall cease,
> And firm, on freedom's base, be fixt an empire's peace.

For, as Milton continues in Sonnet 15 to Lord Thomas
Fairfax, "what can Warrs but endless warr still breed,/Till
Truth, and Right from Violence be freed,/And Public
Fraud. In vain doth Valour bleed/While Avarice, and
Rapine share the land." Milton's poem deals with the
ending of the civil wars in England, and Mason's with the
fraternal strife of the "Sister sov'reign[s] of the wave."
Mason's poem read should not bring detraction; Mason's
poem reread with our recognition of its Miltonic substructs
is placed into a larger poetic and ideological world, and it
may just strike many as integrating reason and imagination
with more than admiration for its poetic source.

"Musæus: A Monody to the Memory of Mr. Pope. In
Imitation of Milton's *Lycidas*" does exhibit much closeness to lines, development, and prosody (the last stanza
is ottava rima, for example), but it also offers a series of
mourners (not unlike Shelley's "Adonais") who recapitulate
the major authors of pastoral elegiacs—the Sicilian Muse
(suggesting Theocritus, Moschus, Vergil, presented in the
meter and rhyming of "Lycidas"), Chaucer as Tityrus,
Spenser as Colin Clout, Milton as Thyrsis. Tityrus speaks
in his archaic language as in "The Hous of Fame"; Colin
Clout speaks of pastoral in two stanzas, as in the January
eclogue of "The Shepheardes Calender," and of fable in

81

three Spenserian stanzas, as in *The Faerie Queene*; Thyrsis, referring to matters in *Paradise Lost*, talks also of "rhyme subdued" in blank verse. Musæus interrupts in heroic couplets with Popean echoes, before the poetic voice returns in the cadences and language of "Lycidas." The poem is strongly Miltonesque. Is it too close an imitation to be no more than appreciation? Or does it encapsulate the traditions of pastoral elegy so differently and so meaningfully that it provides for praise of craft? Is it so derivative that expected sincerity of emotion and loss is impossible? Or is it perhaps apostrophe to Pope more strongly expressed by this parade of mourners, by Musæus's still urging that "all that is is right," by the poet's closing renditions of lines from Vergil's fifth and tenth eclogues, and finally his ceasing of his stripling art and weak dalliance along with morning's end without— in contrast to the imitated ending—any hint of fresh woods or pastures new: "They ceas'd, and with them ceas'd the shepherd swain." It is not poetry of vision, but it is poetry dramatizing the author as a performer.

We have looked at three odes and a pastoral elegy that have received both praise and some negative criticism, all influenced by Milton's poems. Though odes are very frequent in the eighteenth century, ranging from Pindaric and Horatian types as well as the so-called English form (one might think of Joseph Warton's well-known "Ode to Fancy," influenced as it is by Milton's companion poems), the major achievements in odic form of the earlier and later Romantics have perhaps closer precedent in those poems that Wordsworth and Coleridge may have read as schoolboys, an ode like Sir Samuel Egerton Brydges's "To Spring," for instance. It appears as No. IV in *Sonnets and Other Poems* from 1785; when Wordsworth was 15 and Coleridge was 13.

But we should also note the continued writing of son-

nets during the century, despite Samuel Johnson's vitriol-
ic dismissal of the form and despite the unfounded belief
of some literary histories that it had almost disappeared
before the Romantics. We too easily dismiss Thomas
Edwards and ignore Thomas Gray's work in the subgenre,
or think of William Lisle Bowles as not really eighteenth century. Again Brydges's volume offers typical
examples that may have been read by Coleridge or
may have influenced Wordsworth. One instance is
"Sonnet. Written November 30, 1784," a meditation on
his world as he becomes older, though achievement has
thus far passed him by. That it is not an uncommon form
we see from "Sonnet in the Manner of Milton" by an M.
H. P. R. in *The European Magazine* in 1786; or from an
important practitioner like Charlotte Smith, whose
Elegiac Sonnets first appeared in 1784. One of these may
suffice to illustrate her often personal, individual-
centered poems (with a tone and effect similar to
some of Wordsworth's), "Sonnet XII. Written on the Sea
Shore—October 1784":[19]

> On some rude fragment of the rocky shore,
>   Where on the fractured cliff the billows break,
>   Musing, my solitary seat I take,
> And listen to the deep and solemn roar.
> O'er the dark waves the winds tempestuous howl;
>   The screaming sea-bird quits the troubled sea;
>   But the wild gloomy scene has charms for me,
> And suits the mournful temper of my soul.
> Already shipwreck'd by the storms of Fate,
>   Like the poor mariner methinks I stand,
>   Cast on a rock, who sees the distant land
> From whence no succour comes—or comes too late.
> Faint and more faint are heard his feeble cries,
> 'Till in the rising tide the exhausted sufferer dies.

And like the call of Wordsworth in the 1800 Preface, two further sonnets written in 1790 concern "The Sleeping Woodman" and an "image of man and nature," "Written in Passing by Moon-light through a Village, While the Ground was Covered with Snow." Here we find lines like: "In tranquil sleep the village labourers rest," "Hush'd is the hamlet now, and faintly gleam/The dying embers, from the casement low/Of the thatch'd cottage."

Or to understand better what existed poetically prior to *Lyrical Ballads*, we might mention Anne Yearsley, a Milkwoman of Bristol, as the edition of her poems in 1785 has it (in 1787 she is "A Milkwoman of Clifton, near Bristol"). "A Fragment" begins,

> My soul is out of tune,
> No harmony reigns here, 'tis discord all:
> Be dumb, sweet Choristers, I heed you not;
> Then why thus swell your liquid throats, to cheer
> A wretch undone, for ever lost to joy,
> And mark'd for ruin? Seek you leafy grove,
> Indulgent bliss there waits you; shun this spot.

We should also note such poems as "Clifton Hill. Written in January 1785" for its "incidents and situations from common life," or "Soliloquy" for its "very language of men," or "Elegy, Written on the Banks of the Avon, where the Author took a last Farewel of her Brother" (added in 1787) for its "language of prose." Edwards, and Gray, and Bowles and Smith, and Yearsley all evidence a strong Miltonic influence, sometimes also with quotation or adaptation of lines and with allusion. These are among the number of poets of the latter eighteenth century who offer examples of those elements that we consider "romantic" but who should not, in my opinion, be trivialized by the term "pre-Romantic." Only a breaking-up of the standard reading patterns and the certainly outdated critical attitudes is going to allow that statement to be valorized.

To complete this chapter, I would thus like to glance at a few sonnets and poems by Anna Seward, which specifically indicate triumphs of Miltonesque eighteenth century poetry, paving the way for more usually thought of Romantic works.

In her sonnets Seward reflects a reading and understanding of Milton's poetry, both in craft and in substance. Typical are Sonnet XXIII with birds "Choiring the hours of prime" (*PL* 5.170); Sonnet LXVII "On Doctor Johnson's Unjust Criticisms in his Lives of the Poets," with its negative references to *Paradise Lost* and "Lycidas" noted; Sonnet LXXIV, which begins, "In sultry noon when youthful MILTON lay,/Supinely stretch'd beneath the poplar shade," with reference to the Italian sonnets; and Sonnet LXXVIII with its "storied galleries" adapted from "Il Penseroso," "And storied windows richly dight." These, like Milton's, are Petrarchan, and Sonnet LXIV "To Mr Henry Cary, on the Publication of his Sonnets," displaces the volta, as so many of Milton's did, putting it in the middle of line 8, at which time Milton himself is introduced: "—and that heir of fame,/Our greater MILTON"; and as in Milton's poems, enjambment is high—seven out of the 14 lines. The poem itself is a commendation of the sonnet as form and as disciplining craft:

> Prais'd be the Poet, who the Sonnet's claim,
> > Severest of the orders that belong
> > Distinct and separate to the Delphic song,
> > Shall venerate, nor its appropriate name
> Lawless assume. Peculiar is its frame,
> > From him derived, who shunn'd the city throng,
> > And warbled sweet thy rocks and streams among,
> > Lonely Valclusa!—and that heir of fame,
> Our greater MILTON, hath, by many a lay
> > Form'd on that arduous model, fully shown
> > That English verse may happily display

> Those strict energic measures, which alone
> Deserve the name of Sonnet, and convey
> A grandeur, grace and spirit, all their own.

It is a direct rebuttal of Johnson's incompetent statement that "The fabrick of a sonnet, however adapted to the Italian language, has never succeeded in ours, which, having greater variety of termination, requires the rhymes to be often changed." Of Milton's all he could say was "they are not bad," and then modify that by adding "perhaps only the eighth and the twenty-first are truly entitled to this slender commendation." (One may be reminded of Wordsworth's sonnet "Scorn Not the Sonnet," written in 1827, and his lament that Milton "blew/Soul-animating strains—alas, too few!")

Seward's three-quatrain verse "To Miss Godfrey, with Mr Hayley's Life of Milton," illustrates well Milton's happy influence on a sensitive and talented author. Again her negative criticism is directed to Johnson's "Life of Milton," which is obliquely referred to as contrast to William Hayley's admiring one. The truth and eloquence of Hayley's pages make "injustice' dark and transient stain" recede "from that excellence of mind and heart/ Which seated MILTON high in Honour's fane." Her companion poem to Godfrey's sister, the Marchioness of Donegall, talks of "Truth, resistless as Ithuriel's spear," "and detractive powers,/Satanic influence breath'd in Eden's bowers." Both poems attribute Johnson's position to sophistry ("the sophist snares/That wilder judgment in their artful maze," and "party-prejudice, malignant spleen,/And literary envy . . . sophist reasoning"). And perhaps it has been sophistry that has condemned some eighteenth century poetry, influenced by Milton or not, as failure, a sophistry built upon inadequate reading or prejudged reading or expectations for a poem that were not the author's— the fault may lie, not in the writing, but in the critic.

FIVE

Milton and Some
Eighteenth Century
Novels

W hen Louisa is led to the couch by the young lord in
the middle of John Cleland's *Memoires of a Lady of
Pleasure* (1747–48), she goes "nothing loath." We are well
aware that she is far from innocent from her recent account of her life, and we read in those two words that she
not only has no misgivings about the sexual intercourse
about to take place for the surrounding voyeurs, but that
she is quite happy and eager to participate. "The girl,
spreading herself to the best advantage, with her head
upon the pillow, was so concentered in what she was
about," we are told, that the others' presence "seemed the
least of her care and concern." Yet the fiction is that she
is inexperienced. The words "nothing loath" are an allusion, of course, an allusion that creates an intertextuality that works two ways. It attests to the importance
of reading more than just a plain text, despite critical

statements that one keeps hearing; and it attests to what an allusion should be: the reconstruction of a context, insofar as it relates to the particular usage of that allusion, for the deeper understanding of the current context and the intentions of the author. The author *is* a presence in the work through such intertextuality, no matter how long dead he or she may be.

Here the allusion is to John Milton's *Paradise Lost,* book 9, line 1039, when, after Eve and Adam have partaken of the Tree of Good and Evil and have come into knowledge of carnal desire, lasciviousness, and dalliance, "her hand he seis'd, and to a shadie bank,/ . . . He led her nothing loath," "There they thir fill of Love and Loves disport/Took largely." The allusion first comments upon the supposed innocence of Louisa, like Eve, whom "Adam 'gan . . . to dalliance move," except that Eve "well understood" his "amorous intent" and her "Eye darted contagious fire." The allusion has the effect of making all such seductions types of the original fall for the knowledgeable reader, but it also invites the reader to understand Cleland's attitudes concerning such matters. Louisa led her suitor on just as Eve had given Adam "of that fair enticing Fruit/With liberal hand." However, Cleland and most readers of Milton's poem, it seems, forget that Adam "scrupl'd not to eat/Against his better knowledge, not deceav'd." While Milton's Adam realized what he was doing, "fondly overcame with Femal charm," other men, including Cleland, and some women too, chalk the whole fault up to Eve, making Milton a misogynist and a "bogey."

The allusion in *Memoires of a Lady of Pleasure* assures us of how Cleland read Milton's poem and how he knew his perceptive reader would interpret the allusion; Louisa/Eve is but an enticer of false mien, deceptive language, and insidious intent: she is woman, the cause of man's damnation. But in Milton's poem we should remember that

Eve has fallen *before* this scene takes place and so she well understands Adam's intent; and we should remember that Adam has fallen just before these words are said, and thus means more than make love as in the past when he says "now let us play" or when he "forbore not glance or toy/Of amorous intent." The word "play" is the Hebrew *saheq*, with its orgiastic connotations, important particularly when the Israelites, having passed over the Red Sea and entered the wilderness, enjoyed a secure life and took the golden calf as idol: "And they rose up early on the morrow, and offered burnt offerings, and brought peace offerings; and the people sat down to eat and to drink, and rose up to play" (Exod. 22.6).

But Cleland has built in another allusion here, which he may or may not have comprehended fully. Our first views of Adam and Eve see them hand in hand, and the image occurs idyllically in such lines as those depicting the squaring of the circle, a supposed impossibility:

> Rais'd of grassie terf
> Thir Table was, and mossie seats had round,
> And on her ample Square from side to side
> All *Autumn* pil'd, though S*pring* and *Autumn* here
> Danc'd hand in hand.
>
> (5.391–95)

Toward the beginning of book 9, "from her Husbands hand her hand/Soft she withdraw," and of course the temptation and fall then proceed. Her hand Adam *seizes* (a word of some violence) after the fall, and she goes *nothing loath*. Only when "They hand in hand with wandring steps and slow," take their solitary way through Eden, have they returned to the oneness of book 4. Cleland recalls that lustfulness of the seized hand for us, but with no suggestion that any alliance of this woman of pleasure could

89

ever achieve oneness with a lover, for she is the male chauvinist's deceitful woman.

That John Milton was a major influence on eighteenth century literature and religious ideas is a well-known and often repeated belief. There were, as we have said in chapter three, numerous imitations of the versification of *Paradise Lost* through poems in blank verse (often called "Miltonicks") and of *L'Allegro* and *Il Penseroso* in poems employing octosyllabic couplets; the diction, language, imagery of these three poems and of *A Mask* (that is, *Comus*, as the eighteenth century renamed it) constantly reemerged along with appropriations and pointed allusions in the poetry of the century. Dustin Griffin, we have noted, counters the generally alleged deleterious influence of Milton by a more informed and more sympathetic view of eighteenth century poetry. "While, admittedly, second-rate writers seized on superficial or merely technical features of Milton's works, his blank verse prosody or octosyllabic measure, his Latinate diction or his inverted syntax," Griffin explains, "greater writers saw deeper and found inspiration in Milton's great myth of a lost garden of innocence, in his recurrent and related themes of freedom, choice, and responsibility, his celebration of marriage, his defiant stance against his detractors."[1]

However, the area of Milton's importance within the century that remains only briefly touched upon in discussions of a few of the major examples is the novel. I would here like to look briefly at other novels written in the century that reflect Milton's influence in varied ways. The issue of woman in a man's world is often positively seen in the employment of Milton, despite the negative press that he has received at the uninformed hands of some recent feminists; a good corrective is Joseph A. Wittreich's recent *Feminist Milton* (1987).[2]

A novel like *Munster Village* (1778) by Mary Walker, Lady Hamilton, demonstrates the thrust of Wittreich's

book: women authors of the eighteenth century read
Milton approvingly and employed his works in contend-
ing feminist issues. Here Lady Hamilton has Lucy Lee
write to Lady Frances Finlay Munster:

> I am determined never to return to my husband—I have
> consulted my reason on this subject . . . [H]e who follows
> that guide in the search of truth, as that was given to direct
> him, will have a much better plea to make for his conduct,
> than he who has resigned himself implicitly to the gui-
> dance of others. My maxim is, our understanding, *properly*
> exercised, is the *medium* by which God makes known his
> *will* to us; and that in all cases, the voice of impartial reason
> is the voice of God. Were my marriage even to be annulled,
> all the theologians in the world could not prove the least
> impiety in it—Milton wrote the *doctrine and discipline of
> divorce*, wherein he proves, that a contrariety of mind, de-
> structive of felicity, place, and happiness, are greater rea-
> sons of divorce than adultery, especially if there be no
> children, and there be a mutual consent for separation.
>
> He dedicated the second edition to the parliament of
> England, with the assembly of divines—the latter sum-
> moned him before the house of Lords, who, whether ap-
> proving his doctrine, or not favouring his accusers, dis-
> missed him. Necessary and just causes have necessary and
> just consequences: what error and disaster *joined*, reason
> and equity should disjoin.
>
> I see no reason why those who upon the evidence of more
> than fourteen years experience are unsuited to each other,
> *joined* not *matched*, should live disagreeably together, and
> exist miserably—merely for the inadequate satisfaction of
> exulting upon the degree of their patience in having to say
> they did *not part.*

Her reasoning and language, not only the specific
allusion, are Milton's. She rejects reconciliation, but Lady
Frances raises the issue of Scripture, referring to Mark
10.12, Luke 16.18, and Romans 7.3, as invalidating

Mrs. Lee's opinion. The presentation of Mr. Lee in this epistolary novel offers a charming enough but definitely malely superior-thinking person: "None of Mr. Lee's conduct was founded on propriety—he was witty, kind, cold, angry, easy, stiff, jealous, careless, cautious, confident, close, open, but all *in the wrong place*." Lee's alienation from his wife, his impatience, and his extreme gambling underscore the problems of arranged marriages, and so Mrs. Lee's and Mr. Villars's attraction for each other is understandable, though it leads to Mr. Lee's suspecting her virtue, wounding Villars in a duel, and ruining her reputation. For "Mrs. Lee experienced the malevolence of her own sex particularly." Lady Hamilton has put in a gamut of issues concerned with male/female relationships in marriage and in society, presenting a feminist position as well as a good picture of male attitudes and gender separation and of female docility in accepting such gender separation, particularly when the Bible has offered supposedly pertinent admonitions.

Lady Hamilton has clearly read Milton's divorce tracts, it seems, with clear understanding not only that divorce should be allowed for incompatibility, and not only that women as well as men should avail themselves of such recourse, but also that the biblists are led by preconceptions. For we remember that Milton in *Tetrachordon* dealt with the four places in Scripture that talk of marriage and the nullities of marriage and turned his interpretations of God's and Jesus' words into acceptable arguments for divorce.

These themes and gender attitudes emerge in numerous novels of the times. In *The Sisters; or, The History of Lucy and Caroline Sanson, entrusted to a False Friend* (1786) Mr. Dookalb tells Caroline that "the Scripture promises temporal rewards to nothing more certainly than obedience to parents." She, deceived by his appearance of being one of the very best of men—with purposes that are all just, friendly, and pure—yields. But the anonymous author remarks, "no wonder that he, whose hypocrisy passed undiscovered by many far wiser, could conceal his soul from a poor weak woman," and quotes Milton on Uriel's deception by Satan: "For neither Man nor Angel can discern/Hypocrisie, the only evil that walks/Invisible, except to God alone." Captain Smith has a liaison with Lucy, and we are told of his partially undressing her, and then: "Thus fell the unhappy daughter of an unhappy father, from her state of innocence and joy; like our first mother, seduced and betrayed, who fatally *plucked* and *eat*," and the passage beginning, "her rash hand in evil hour" is then quoted. Of Lucy, attending a play at Miss Charlotte's insistence (with thus the moralistic attitude toward plays and playgoing being implied), the author writes that "mixing much endearing blandishments, and many very alleviating circumstances, (as, when did woman in such a case want an advocate?) the fond captain was soon softened, and won over, like our first father," and *Paradise Lost* 9.999 ff., referenced in a footnote, is quoted. This is the point where Adam falls. "So was it with our no less fallen, lost, and miserable couple: they burnt with lust; their eyes darted contagious fire, and their wanton purposes were not long unexecuted— 'They their full of love and love's disport/Took largely, of thir mutual guilt the Seal,/The solace of thir sin, till dewie sleep/Oppress'd them, wearied with thir amorous play."

Lucy's real love, however, is Mr. Leicart, and when Mary Steele views them she is likened to Satan first observing Adam and Eve. We have "true" love thus contrasted with the lust depicted before. Is the author recording reality? is he or she recording reality made memorable by Milton? is the author not exhibiting male attitudes toward women, and thereby not reading Milton very carefully?

The very interesting Jane West plays on the ambivalence that Milton and his works could provide. In *The Advantages of Education, or, The History of Maria Williams, A Tale for Misses and Their Mammas* (1793), appalled at the idleness of the boarding school girl who is dressed in high fashion, she notes that they, "instructed only to dance, 'To dress, to troll the tongue, and roll the eye,' Are by Milton affirmed to be destitute of all good, wherein consists 'Woman's domestic honour, and chief praise.'" This digression in her tale is concerned with "the rage for idleness (I beg pardon, I mean refinement; I always mistake those words) . . . ." In *A Tale of the Times* (1799) she quotes or references *L'Allegro*, the Limbo of Vanity (that is "the modern Parnassus"), "the arch Apostate . . . on viewing Adam and Eve in Paradise" (this being Mr. Fitzosborne in reference to the Monteiths), *Comus*, and the frequently cited "Hail wedded Love." I find 13 specific uses of Milton to further West's story or character analysis or to suggest a frame of mind for reading the ensuing chapter. In *A Gossip's Story* (1798), she also employs *Lycidas* as Mrs. Dudley's daughter clears decaying branches from a rose bush planted by her mother and thus "indulged the pleasing melancholy which a departed friend impresses upon the memory, when time has softened the agonies of grief into mild regret and pious resignation." Her melancholy immediately leads to her composing an elegiac sonnet on a rose bush. Indeed, I find often that the poetry served up by authors of novels in the eighteenth century illustrates Miltonic influence, not only in such forms as the sonnet (which certainly did not die during the century) but in imagery and language. Sir Samuel Egerton Brydges, who later became an editor of Milton's works, is one instance in his *Arthur Fitz-Albini, A Novel* (1798), which also quotes or alludes to Milton specifically three times.

Mary Wollstonecraft's *Mary, A Fiction* (1788) reflects her enthusiasm for Milton, just as *A Vindication of The Rights of Woman* does when the full work is read and Milton's pervasive importance recognized. The novel cites or quotes *L'Allegro* or *Paradise Lost* in chapters 2, 4, 17, 18, and 19. In Chapter 18, Mary, engaged through family and financial concerns to a man she dislikes, meets Henry and is attracted to him. Her affections, she says, are involuntary to all, adapting in her argument for sensibility *Paradise Lost* 8.591–92: "That earthly love is the scale by which to heavenly we may ascend." The context that Wollstonecraft wants her reader to evoke is Raphael's admonishment of Adam, who shows himself to be intemperately enamoured of Eve—"All higher knowledge in her presence falls/Degraded." Raphael counters:

What higher in her societie thou findst
Attractive, human, rational, love still;
In loving thou dost well, in passion not,
Wherein true Love consists not; love refines
The thoughts, and heart enlarges, hath his seat
In Reason, and is judicious, is the scale
By which to heav'nly Love thou maist ascend,
Not sunk in carnal pleasure. . . .

Wollstonecraft, unlike Cleland, has seen Milton's Adam's failing in this precursor to the Fall and Milton's Raphael's idealistic view of woman and man's love.

But Milton's presence in eighteenth century novels covers more than the Eve/Adam question. In *Tom Jones* there is the invocation to book 13 with its language and apostrophe straight out of the epic:

Come, bright love of fame, inspire my glowing breast: not thee I call, who, over swelling tides of blood and tears, dost bear the hero on to glory, while sighs of millions waft his spreading sails; but thee, fair, gentle maid, whom Mnesis, happy nymph, first on the banks of Hebrus did produce. . . . And thou, much plumper dame, . . . Instructed by thee, some books, like quacks, impose on the world by promising wonders, ... And now this ill-yoked pair, this lean shadow and this fat substance, have prompted me to write, whose assistance shall I invoke to direct my pen?

Frances Brooke has her Arabella Fermor describe Canada thus, in letter 10 of *The History of Emily Montague* (1769): "I am at present at an extreme pretty farm on the banks of the river St. Lawrence; the house stands at the foot of a steep mountain covered with a variety of trees, forming a verdant sloping wall, which rises on a kind of regular confusion, 'Shade above shade, a woody theatre,' " a quotation of *Paradise Lost* 4.141, a line in the midst of the first description of Eden, which thus directs the knowing reader to view Canada as offering the Edenic life as she continues: "I never saw a place so found to inspire that pleasing lassitude, that divine inclination to saunter, which may not improperly be called, the luxurious indolence of the country. I intend to build a temple here to the charming goddess of laziness." Brooke was indeed well learned in Milton's works, as issues of *The Old Maid* show, or as letter 167 does in its quotation of Milton's translation out of all the other possible translations of Horace's Fifth Ode: "His dank and dropping weeds/To the stern god of sea."

Or one might look at Samuel Richardson's *The History of Sir Charles Grandison*, for example, letter 13 in volume 1, in which Harriet sets forth the positive and negative arguments over Milton's learning and sublimity to conclude that "If Homer is to be preferred to Milton, he must be the sublimest of writers; and Mr. Pope, admirable as his translation of the *Iliad* is said to be, cannot have done him justice." Structures and issues drawn from *Paradise Lost* inform the journey and quest of Samuel Johnson's *Rasselas*; from *Comus*, William Godwin's *Imogen*. Godwin's view of Satan in *Political Justice*[3] underlies his portrait of Falkland as the unjust God in *Caleb Williams* and paves the way for Mary Shelley's *Frankenstein* and the Monster. As Caleb says in chapter 6 of the second volume, "My offence had merely been a mistaken thirst of knowledge," uniting Satan and Adam as the pawns of the unjust God. Caleb, in chapter 10, will not fall down at the feet of one who is to him a devil, or kiss the hand that is red with his blood; he is, to Mr. Forester, a serpent, a monster of ingratitude. He goes into voluntary banishment from his native land, in chapter 15 of the third volume and promises to tell a tale to become "triumphant, and crush his seemingly omnipotent foe." Godwin uses Milton's Satan's words in the Postscript to describe Falkland, "firm in command and capable to extort obedience from every one that approached him." And it is Caleb who extends the expected mercy of the godhead: "Thy intellectual powers were truly sublime, and thy bosom burned with a godlike ambition. But of what use are talents and sentiments in the corrupt wilderness of human society?"

But an author who seems to be read enthusiastically only by a dedicated coterie, yet who knew Milton and his works very well, is William Beckford. Milton supplies descriptions, particularly of geographic and natural worlds; ironic and satiric reversals; the means to humor and critical stances—and from a wide variety of sources. In his *Italy; With Sketches of Spain and Portugal*, though not of course a novel, in letter 31, on 19 October 1787, discussing the mountains of Cintra, Beckford writes:

> As I was doomed to be disturbed and talked out of the elysium in which I had been lapped for these last seven or eight hours, it was no matter . . . and away we galloped. The

horses were remarkably sure-footed, or else, I think, we must have rolled down the precipices; for our road, 'If road it could be call'd where road was none,' led us by zigzags and short cuts over steeps and acclivities about three or four leagues, till reaching a healthy desert, where a solitary cross staring out of a few weather-beaten bushes, marked the highest point of this wild eminence, one of the most expansive prospects of sea, and plain, and distant mountains, I ever beheld, burst suddenly upon me, rendered still more vast, aereal, and indefinite, by the visionary, magic vapour of the evening sun.

The adaptation is of the first line describing Death in book 2 of *Paradise Lost*. Beckford has, for the informed, contrasted his elysium with hell and the geography with an abode of death, giving added meaning to "vast, aereal, and indefinite, by the visionary, magic vapour of the evening sun," with its added allusion to the desiccation that ends the epic.

His *Modern Novel Writing, or the Elegant Enthusiast; and Interesting Emotions of Arabella Bloomville. A Rhapsodical Romance: Interspersed with Poetry* (1796), supposedly by the Right Honorable Lady Harriet Marlow, has Amelia tell Arabella her story of Don Pedro de Gonzales, whose possessive love she wants to flee. Don Pedro sees Captain Beville kissing Amelia, runs him through, and she flees and then exclaims *Comus*, 180–85, with deliberate inaccuracies:

> O where else
> Shall I *deform* my *unattainted* feet,
> In the blind *masses* of this *dangled* wood?
> For I am wearied out
> With the long way *resolving* here to lodge
> Under the spreading *favour* of these pines.

"Arabella seizing time by the foreclock, led her new acquaintance to the woodbine bower, which amorous innocence had wove for contemplation and repose." Beckford has the reader juxtaposing the innocent Lady about to be accosted by Comus, and Eve in the bower that has been made for Adam (the significance of "contemplation" here) and for Eve apparently in her softness and sweet attractive grace (as 4.297–98, would imply). And thus with that word "repose" we're back with woman as sex object.

The postscript to this novel about modern novel writing jibes *The British Critic's* moralistic criticism, if such funning as the preceding hasn't already made the reader certain that Arabella only appears to be a "Pensive Nun devout and pure,/Sober, steadfast and demure," with the comment, "But to lay aside all levity, it is impossible to deny that you waste your midnight oil, to save the present race from the horrors of licentiousness and the encroachments of philosophy."

Milton is simply ubiquitous in these novels, whether seriously or satirically employed to communicate to the knowing reader an intertext that may say much about the author and the author's attitudes.

SIX

Narrative Strategies in Eighteenth Century Women's Fiction

O nly recently have novels of the eighteenth century written by women been given very much attention, but even so they have often, it seems, been considered in relation to novels written by men. At a 1989 conference when narratological approaches in eighteenth century fiction were discussed in broad, all-inclusive terms, I heard no awareness that novels of the period written by women might not be confined to the generalizations that were being offered. As I look over some of those texts, which are unfortunately little known as yet (except for those by Fanny Burney and Maria Edgeworth) and which are going to continue to be placed in a kind of inferior position because they are not necessarily doing what Defoe, Richardson, Fielding, and Smollett did, I believe

I see narrative strategies, and other strategies, that lead to a different reading experience. I confine my remarks here to that latter group by looking at a few examples: Elizabeth Haywood's *The Agreeable Caledonian: or, Memoirs of Signiora di Morella, a Roman Lady* (1728), Frances Brooke's *The History of Lady Julia Mandeville* (1763), Mary Walker, Lady Hamilton's *Letters from the Duchess de Crui and Others, on Subjects Moral and Entertaining* (1776), her *Munster Village* (1778), and Mary Wollstonecraft's *Mary* (1788). Many other novels could have been chosen for discussion, yielding like examples.

From the beginning of prose narratives in English, the epistolary form has been employed, as in George Gascoigne's *The Adventures of Master F. J.* (1573), one of the first, if not the first, English "novel." He, like other earlier practitioners, also fills his prose with poems. Later, while the backbone of a narrative continues to be letters, an omniscient narrative voice unites these epistles by comment and provision of "story" lines. It is clear that such prose narratives may have an episodic quality, not dissimilar to such early examples as Thomas Deloney's tales (1596–1600), and indeed that some may reflect "rogue" literature in the vein of Richard Head's *The English Rogue* (1666–71). But well before Samuel Richardson wrote, other novelists were providing a continuous and psychologically oriented narrative, often epistolary and therefore somewhat episodic, often with poetry included, and often character-important rather than story-important, once the reader sees that the protagonist is not necessarily following a path that is expected.

A case in point is Haywood's "novel," Part 1, in which the protagonist, Clementina di Morella, is first seen as a woman subject to paternal (and male) controls, and then as a woman subject to scandalous inference. Her rejection of such controls and her attempt to pursue her own romantic attachment (even though she is not truly happy with Bellario) cause her to be "destin'd to bewail her Disobedience" in the Cloister of the Augustines at Viterbo. In the course of the novel, which is punctuated by epistles and poetry, Clementina becomes friends with fellow cloister resident Miramene, who is in love with Glencairn, the agreeable Scot. Clementina plans a means by which the lovers may meet. But meeting him herself, she effects a change, separating the two and getting Glencairn for herself, by dishonest means, lying and false implications. Glencairn rescues her from the convent, and the novel ends.

A reader, of course, has not expected a *woman* of high position to be so manipulative and so unscrupulous: her morality is to be questioned and has been by the few critics who have written anything about this work. Perhaps in the reader's eyes she has joined such "low-caste" people as Moll Flanders or (later) Fanny Hill. But a reading of this work as simply a "moral romance," regardless of the critic's understanding of the psychological portrait being presented, is, I feel, to misread it. The strategy that Haywood uses to achieve reader recognition of attitudes toward the sexes—which for me is a major, if not the major, subject of the narrative—is to put circumstances at an extreme to make the point. That is a frequent strategy in much argumentative writing, and it should set up here the rejection of the usual concept of the "moral" woman as being male-generated, once we make the comparison. Mr. B. may take on the sentimental mask of reformed rake and thereby be acceptable as consort for the honest and steadfast Pamela, but Haywood had already shown more than a decade earlier that woman can be heroine and assert herself above paternal domination, above male-generated affiliations, and above female passivity. Part 2 hedges, but Part 1 makes clear that morality or its abnegation should not be defined along sexual lines.

A careful reading of Milton's Eve makes the same point. The "separation" scene of book 9 of *Paradise Lost* indicates not defiance of the woman but commendable reasoning and action (rather than mere passivity), even though it sets the stage for the fraudulence of Satan to exert itself. And it is Eve who leads the reconciliation with Adam and the repentance through recognition of her role in the protevangelium. Eve is the last person to speak in the poem, a most notable position, and her words iterate the significance of her womanly role in the ultimate defeat of Satan.

Indeed, in Haywood's *The Agreeable Caledonian*, it is Glencairn who presents a very normal and good person, one who has been manipulated, though he is surely not a fool. And part of Haywood's narrative strategy is to present a "life history" of Miramene which parallels the usual female history of family and true love. Sentimentally we want Miramene to find happiness with her loving Baron; she is so good, so honest and straightforward, so like so many women in "moral romances." She says to Clementina, "But I am certain, so much do I depend on the Sincerity of my dear Baron, that it will never cease thro' any Fault of his; and so happy do I make myself in the Assurance of his Love, that I would not exchange Conditions with an Empress." Of course, she is right: he accepts Clementina soon afterward not through any fault of his. Haywood is setting the reader up to fall into that trap of commonplace sentimentality, to condemn Clementina, to say of the agreeable Scot "the poor schnook."

The epigraph on the title page and the title page itself emphasize the subject of the novel as love, specifically Clementina's love of Glencairn, and ends "But Fortune took the Part of Love, and disappointed all the Endeavours made to separate the Bodies of two Persons, whose Hearts were at present united by the fondest and most violent Affection that ever was the Theme of History." The narrative offers us a psychological picture of a woman caught in a patriarchal society, a woman who develops as a person unwilling to be but passive, who rejects the usual male-generated love affair, who brings into reality a love affair desirable to *her*, and who is not above ruses. One such ruse is to encourage Glencairn's continued pursuit of Miramene in a postscript after insinuating her own favor in his eyes: "I was half-tempted to believed, I seem'd indeed not less lovely in your Eyes than *Miramene* had been.—Time and your future Behavior alone will make it appear which of these various Conjectures had most of Truth.—I permit you to give me the Confirmation," she writes to him and in the postscript adds, "Whatever in Reality are your Sentiments of me, I entreat you will not omit writing to *Miramene*." Perhaps the male chauvinist is saying, "Just like an entrapping woman!" but the portrait also leads to a conclusion that Haywood is asserting woman's right, if it is man's right, to direct the game of love, to become the director of her own fate. The novel is surely character-important.

This oppositional view of the man/woman, love/ marriage condition is a main concern of Mary Walker, Lady Hamilton's novel *Munster Village*, which we have looked at in chapter five. Again we have an epistolary, and again action is taken by a woman but questioned by another woman who reflects the usual societal thinking in pointing out the problems that may ensue by such action. Here the narrative strategy is to offer logic and theoretical precedence for a divorce action by Lucy Lee and to have Lady Munster rebut it by recourse to Scripture, the last infirmity of conventional mind, I might suggest. This is only one episode in the novel, but an important one as far as feminist issues and the novel are concerned, as the quotation on pp. 109–10 evinces. It was uncommon to present a woman who really thinks, who displays reason, and who has not "resigned herself implicitly to the guidance of others." But even more uncommon is Lee's backing up her position by a kind of authorizing precedent and by a justification of divorce well ahead of its time and only in rather recent years generally accepted, that is, incompatibility. Walker likewise lampoons the verbiage of the wedding ceremony here: "what error and disaster joined, reason and equity should disjoin."

A woman who has read something other than "Poems for Young Ladies?" a woman who thinks and extrapolates to specific situations? a woman who can decipher differing meanings in language?—here is someone different from Roxana or Clarissa or Amelia. The great significance of this portrait presented in this way is underscored by the charming but definitely malely superior-thinking person of Mr. Lee: "None of Mr. Lee's conduct was founded on propriety—he was witty, kind, cold, angry, easy, stiff, jealous, careless, cautious, confident, close, open, but all *in the wrong places*." We today would wonder why she stayed with him as long as she did, for his alienation from his wife, his impatience, and his extreme gambling indict this arranged marriage. Her finding consolation in Mr. Villar's mutual attraction adds another more modern touch, but leads to the continuing assumption that in such cases virtue is to be suspect and to cause the ruin of a reputation thereby.

Yet another important strategy that Walker uses is to have Lady Munster gently reprove Mrs. Lee by suggesting first reconciliation and then invalidation of divorce as solution on the basis of Mark 10.12, Luke 16.18, and Romans 7.3. The polite and proper rejection of divorce— that is, rejection of a woman's taking a definite action for her own welfare—coming from a woman and then on the basis of the words of Jesus and Saint Paul loads the case against feminine thinking and decision and action. That is, if one falls into such conventional attitudes; that is, if one dismisses the person in favor of received belief. But of course the reader is led to reject that rejection of Mrs. Lee's divorce by the development of this whole episode. Indeed, Lee's ruined reputation leads to the comment that "Mrs. Lee experienced the malevolence of her own sex particularly." Walker has put into her novel a gamut of issues concerned with male/female relationships in marriage and in society, presenting a feminist position as well as a good picture of male attitudes and gender separation and of female docility in accepting such gender separation. She does not tell us what to conclude, but we reject Lady Munster's view without thinking the worse of her, only feeling sorry that she should submit to such unenlightened social pressure.

Another strategy Walker employs in *Letters from the Duchess de Crui and Others, on Subjects Moral and Entertaining* is allusive quotation in this strict epistolary. While works like Richardson's *The History of Sir Charles Grandison* or Johnson's *Rasselas* are replete with Miltonic echoes, which at least in the latter provide an intertext, these letters employ references and quotations from *Paradise Lost* (there is also one from *Of Education*) that concentrate on a reading of Eve and Adam, leading to a subtext. The letters are all from women to other women, and what we see in the allusions is a concern with the epitome of Eve with its emphasis on her beauty and grace, and with its apostrophe by Adam before the Fall. The pedestal-placing of Eve by Adam is both reveled in and questioned, and leads to understanding that woman has thus been subordinated to man: "The World lay all before *him*" (my emphasis), Letter 11 in volume 1. As a full epistolary, this novel does not use an omniscient narrator to comment and direct the reader into interpretations. The personalities (and the authorial concerns) can be derived only from what is said and how it is said: aside from inferences about the recipient of a letter, we discern the people of the novel through such allusive quotation.

Frances Moore Brooke, who wrote the periodical *The Old Maid* under the pseudonym Mary Singleton, Spinster, has been credited with reviving the epistolary after Richardson, and became well known as the author of *The History of Emily Montague*, with its sweep of Canadian landscape and rural life. *The History of Lady Julia Mandeville*, an epistolary without authorial unifying comment, warranted seven editions in 12 years. Its story is not bothered by the trite reformed rake motif, and it proceeds with a restrained tone, but one that has a natural air to it, as of ordinary people talking. It provides a setting of society in which sensibility reigns in the everyday life of natural people. Yet its two basic plots are set out almost contrapuntally in two series of letters: one, in which Henry Mandeville loves and is to be married to Julia, is complicated by rumors of a forced marriage with Lord Melvin and a delayed communication telling Henry of his inheritance, ending in his death in a duel with Melvin and Julia's ensuing demise; the other, in which Anne Wilmot must deny marriage to Bellville because of his impoverishment and her late husband's willing his fortune to his niece should she remarry, ends with Bellville's unexpected inheritance. While the sad events of Henry and Julia's deaths are played through the final series of letters, the happy marriage of Anne and Bellville (and of Lord Melvin and Arabella Hastings, Anne Wilmot's cousin and now inheritor of her father's estate) offset the gloom somewhat.

Brooke's strategies are quite different from those of her

immediate predecessors in the novel and most instructive for those who come after her. The natural language, the low-keyed tone, of ordinary life is to emerge in such novels as Fannie Burney's and Jane Austen's; the emphasis on love rather than passion and on sensibility rather than strong action contrasts strongly with Fielding's or Smollett's writings. The articulation of tone and treatment with the stories being told remove episodic feeling; the smooth weaving of the two basic plots and the almost casual introduction of the past maintain that sense of unity. The excision of prolepsis likewise maintains the natural unfolding of a "real" story, rather than creating a "literary" one that pulls us forward with a kind of dramatic irony. I think that Brooke knew very well what she was doing, and I believe that the adverse contemporary criticism of this novel, unhappy with its not following formula, proves me right.[1]

In a way, Wollstonecraft's first novel, *Mary*, seems unfinished, a work partially in process. For it becomes a fictional work only in its not being a biographical memoir, but not because of the substance or its language and tone. We can see Mary Wollstonecraft behind her character Mary, and more importantly we can understand the author's wrestling with questions of woman and her life in the confines of arranged marriage, incompatible marriage, and personal feelings. She did not call this work a novel, perhaps meaningfully; it is "A Fiction." But it is posing the sources of sensibility by its splitting of reality and imagination and creation of the symbolic. Mary and her world are presented to the reader through the being of Mary's mind and feelings speaking out as brief interior monologues:

> In a few days she must again go to sea; the weather was very tempestuous—what of that, the tempest in her soul rendered every other trifling—it was not the contending elements, but *herself* she feared!

Not only is the emotion symbolically presented, an emotion to be felt by many (men as well as women) at various junctures of life, but the imagery of the sea of life upon which one is tossed by confused forces is made to be personal: what tempests occur are related at least to personal forces, not simply outside forces over which we have no control. The thought moves toward the core of Wollstonecraft's achievement in her writing: the need to understand the self, then to reduce those outside forces or alter them or render them innocuous.

The work, like others, tellingly employs allusive quotation, here most often from Edward Young's *Night-Thoughts* and Milton's "L'Allegro" or *Paradise Lost*. Having met Henry and finding a mutual attraction, Mary, in chapter 18, says that her affections are involuntary to all, stressing thus the sensible, and she continues her argument for sensibility by adapting *Paradise Lost* 8.591–92: "That earthly love is the scale by which to heavenly we may ascend." Wollstonecraft wants her reader to evoke Raphael's admonishment of Adam, who has shown himself intemperately enamoured of Eve. She has seen in Adam's failing a precursor to the Fall and in Raphael's lines, idealistic though they are, true love that is not simply bodily. All of this goes to the heart of the question of marriage and personal desires, and particularly for those times, woman's desires. Focusing as she does on Mary, Wollstonecraft enlists the reader's own sensibility to reject the societal commonplaces about women/men.

Her strategies in achieving this are primarily twofold: First, she presents brief interior monologues, as I have noted, truly deep inner thoughts, or if clearly reported by the narrative voice, these monologues take us into Mary's being more effectively than do others' fictions where there is a surface-telling that makes us conscious of an author standing at a distance and reporting. For instance:

> She knelt by the bed side;—an enthusiastic devotion overcame the dictates of despair.—She prayed most ardently to be supported, and dedicated herself to the service of that Being into whose hands, she had committed the spirit she almost adored—again—and again,—she prayed wildly—and fervently—but attempting to touch the lifeless hand—her head swum—she sunk—

Secondly,—and perhaps this strategy, while effective enough, yields an unfinished quality to the whole—she uses little direct quotation, or when she does use it, she makes it clearly reportage. The style may be a considered attempt to move away from the epistolary and to obviate a readership expected to mull over *subjects* raised. Instead it takes that readership into attitudes that should be plumbed for meaning or sensibility. While the fiction is developed by telling rather than by showing, it nonetheless demands a reader who will internalize what is told, as in the following:

> In one thing there seemed to be a sympathy between them, for she wrote formal answers to his as formal letters. An extreme dislike took root in her mind; the sound of his name made her turn sick; but she forgot all, listening to Ann's cough, and supporting her languid frame. She would then catch her to her bosom with convulsive eagerness, as if to save her from sinking into an opening grave.

This paragraph from chapter 6 strikes us at first as dealing with two different matters, but their conjunction is an unavoidable indication of the problem facing Mary: a husband she despises and a mothering that overwhelms the heart and obliterates the mind.[2]

The narrative strategies that can be observed in eighteenth century women novelists are numerous, and they are not necessarily exclusively female. But much of the narratological discourse one hears seems to take substance from only male writers, and so much of the discourse is so theoretically oriented that it seems divorced from the actuality of the writing. The examples cited above aid in pursuing the kind of study Ann Messenger engaged in *His and Hers*,[3] and I hope that they suggest both the importance of the actual authorial text, whether male or female (not just some depersonalized distant view), and the nature of some women's writing in the eighteenth century.

SEVEN

Milton
and the
French Revolution

I f there be one fact in the world perfectly clear, it is this,—"that the disposition of the people of America is wholly averse to any other than a free government"; and this is indication enough to any honest statesman how he ought to adapt whatever power he finds in his hands to their case. If any ask me what a free government is, I answer, that, for any practical purpose, it is what the people think so,—and that they, and not I, are the natural, lawful, and competent judges of this matter. If they practically allow me a greater degree of authority over them than is consistent with any correct ideas of perfect freedom, I ought to thank them for so great a trust, and not to endeavor to prove from thence that they have reasoned amiss, and that, having gone so far, by analogy they must hereafter have no enjoyment but by my pleasure.[1]

Yet the implications of this statement written in 1777 are rejected in 1790 as not applicable to the Revolution of

1688. Richard Price, a Unitarian minister and member of the Revolution Society of London, had talked in 1790 of a general right "to choose our own governors, to cashier them for misconduct, and to form a government for ourselves"[2] in likening the French Revolution to the Glorious English Revolution. These principles are not applicable, it is contended, because they are not found in the Declaration of Right between Parliament and William and Mary, which act declares the rights and liberties of the subject and the succession of the crown. The writer's thinking on the French Revolution can thus be gauged: theirs was not the situation of the American colonies, and approval would be tacit approval of a like disbandment of the English government. "Is our monarchy to be annihilated, with all the laws, all the tribunals, and all the ancient corporations of the kingdom?" he asks. To him the French Revolution is militant; to them, triumphant. Were the king a wicked tyrant, still punishment should have "dignity," justice should be "grave" and "decorous."[3]

We can understand the unspoken text: Edmund Burke, whom I have been quoting, like many English today, is still reacting to the execution of Charles I in 1649, approving certain philosophic concepts and even movements to establish those concepts, but drawing a line where monarchy is concerned. "We have not (as I conceive) lost the generosity and dignity of thinking of the fourteenth century; nor as yet have we subtilized ourselves into savages. We are not the converts of Rousseau; we are not the disciples of Voltaire; Helvitius has made no progress amongst us."[4] But it is the presence of John Milton that hangs over so many of these ideas and attitudes, both the positive ones as in Price and in Burke, and the negative ones, unacknowledged, as also in Burke. Agreement seems to be frequent "That it is Lawfull, and hath been held so through all Ages, for any, who have the Power, to call to account a Tyrant, or wicked King," as the title page of *The Tenure of Kings and Magistrates* proclaims, but the seemingly logical next step is not taken: "and after due conviction, to depose, and put him to death; if the ordinary Magistrate have neglected, or deny'd to doe it." Indeed, Price echoes Milton squarely, "a king is no more than the first servant of the public, created by it, *and responsible to it,*" but to Burke this is direct opposition to "one of the wisest and most beautiful parts of our Constitution."[5]

A major purveyor of these Miltonic thoughts was Algernon Sidney, put to death in December 1683 for his part in the Rye House Plot, both in *The Very Copy of a Paper Delivered to the Sheriffs upon the Scaffold on Tower-Hill,* which quotes directly from Milton's *The Tenure of Kings and Magistrates,* and in *Discourses Concerning Government,* which draws upon the same tract and *Pro populo Anglicano defensio* (that is, *The First Defense*). Sidney's *Discourse* was translated and published into French by P. A. Samson in 1702 and enjoyed a number of editions through the century, with the paper delivered to the sheriffs being added. Indeed, in 1793, after having been forced into hiding by the turn of events, Marie-Jean-Antoine-Nicolas Caritat, Marquis de Condorcet, a major thinker who set the stage for the French Revolution and was largely responsible for the republican constitution presented in early 1793, wrote in the introduction to *A Historical Picture of the Progress of the Human Mind:* "These principles, which the noble Sydney paid for with his blood and on which Locke set the authority of his name, were later developed by Rousseau with greater precision, breadth, and energy, and he deserves renown for having established them among the truths that it is no longer permissible to forget or to combat."[6]

Among those principles are the Miltonic rejection that one group is fated to rule, another to obey, and the Miltonic argument "that all men possess equal rights by nature." Milton, himself not a regicide, although many have so classified him, does not try "to reconcile men's minds" to the execution of Charles I, which was certain when Milton wrote in 1649, and in 1651 after the event. Condorcet had to go into hiding because of his disagreement with the Reign of Terror of July 1793. But his republican principles and his emphasis on education suggest an ultimate Miltonic source. His Constitutional Plan detailed why "Monarchy . . . had to be abolished"; it argued that the French should "follow the example of a people worthy of imitation," the Americans; and it concluded in the language of Rousseau, Montesquieu, Sidney, and Milton: "Thus nature, which has willed that each people preside over its own laws, has decreed equally that all people be the arbiter of its own prosperity and happiness."[7] In *Tenure*, among other places, Milton had written: "Whence doubtless our Ancestors who were not ignorant with what rights either Nature or ancient Constitution had endowd them, when Oaths both at Coronation, and renewd in Parlament would not serve, thought it no way illegal to depose and put to death thir tyrannous Kings," and in *Eikonoklastes:* "I hold reason to be the best Arbitrator, and the Law of Law it self."[8]

Prior to the insurgence of 17 June 1789, led by Emanuel Joseph Sieyès and Honoré Gabriel Riquetti, Comte de Mirabeau, there appeared *Sur la Liberté de la Presse, Imité de l'Anglois, de Milton. Par le Comte de Mirabeau. Who kills a man kills a reasonable creature . . . but he who destroys a good book, kills reason it self.* The French text was published in 1788, twice in 1789, and again in 1792, "premier de la République." We can assume at least an awareness of such Milton works as *Areopagitica* prior to 1788 because of the extensive editions of translations of the poetry, particularly *Paradise Lost* from 1729 onward, and such criticism as that regularly found in journals like *Mercure de France*; and from such lives of the author as Louis Racine's in his translation of the epic in 1755. In 1788 there were two different editions of two different translations of the epic, both with lives, and one with *Paradise Regain'd* and other poems included.

But with the outbreak of resistance and the establishment of the National Assembly in June 1789 and the attack on the Bastille a month later came two different editions of *Théorie de la Royauté, d'Après la Doctrine de Milton*, written by Jean Baptiste Salaville. This is an abbreviated form of *Pro populo Anglicano defensio* in ten chapters. It presents Milton's arguments against monarchy in straightforward language. Much of Milton's argument is against the belief in an analogy of patriarchy and kingship, a son's unquestioning duty to his father, thus a subject's to a king, with an attendant playing upon Jesus's obedience to God the Father—religious creeds often being the instrument to stifle criticism or change. Milton rebuts in the *First Defense* the metaphor that forces one to apply to kings whatever is admitted of fathers:

> Fathers and kings are very different things: Our fathers begot us, but our kings did not, and it is we, rather, who created the king. It is nature which gave the people fathers, and the people who gave themselves a king; the people therefore do not exist for the king, but the king for the people.[9]

A prime adherent of patriarchy was Sir Robert Filmer, whose 1640s text was not published until 1680, though it had circulated in manuscript, but whose *Observations Concerning the Originall of Government*, 1652 and frequently thereafter, reproduced some of Milton's remarks in order to challenge them. It was this work that was a major impetus for John Locke's 1690 *Two Treatises of Government: In the former, the False Principles, and Foundation of Sir Robert Filmer, and His Followers, Are Detected and Overthrown.* It was soon translated into French in 1691 by David Mazel, and the eighteenth century saw numerous reprints, with the title *Du Gouvernement civil, Où l'on traitte de l'Origine, des Fondemens, de la Nature, du Pouvoir & des Fins des Sociétez politiques.*[10]

Following upon such political philosophy of Milton as was encompassed by Sidney and Locke, Jean-Jacques Rousseau reacted strongly to this foregoing issue. In *Discours sur l'origine et les fondements de l'inégalité parmi les hommes* (1753), expanded into *Le Contrat social* in 1762, Rousseau wrote:

> As to paternal authority, from which several have derived absolute government and every other mode of society, it is sufficient, without having recourse to Locke and Sidney, to observe that nothing in the world differs more from the cruel of despotism, than the gentleness of that authority, which looks more to the advantage of him who obeys than to the utility of him who commands; that by the law of nature the father continues master of his child no longer than the child stands in need of his assistance; that after that term they become equal, and that then the son, entirely independent of the father, owes him no obedience, but only respect . . . . Instead of saying the civil society is derived from paternal authority, we should rather say that it is to the former that the latter owes its principal force.[11]

Milton's ideas were certainly present in sources known by political thinkers prior to the French Revolution, and now in 1789 they were directly offered as rationale for the overt action taking place. Just as Milton's *First Defense* was produced under commission from the English Council of State to explain the actions of what became the Cromwellian government and to nullify the position of

Salmasius in *Defensio Regia, Pro Carolo I*, so Salaville's translation served to justify and explain the insurrection and such actions as the National Constitution Assembly's abolition of feudal and manorial privileges on 4 August 1789.

Included as a preface to the translation of the *First Defense* was a 78-page discussion "Sur Milton et ses ouvrages" by Mirabeau. The translation with this long preface appeared again in 1790, and as *Défense du Peuple Anglais, sur le Jugement et la Condamnation de Charges Premier, Roi D'Angleterre, Par Milton* in ?1792, but without Mirabeau's discussion, possibly because Mirabeau had died some months before. Mirabeau discusses various texts and Milton's political philosophy as it coincided with French intellectual governmental philosophy. Additionally, in 1792 a French translation of John Adams's *Défense des Constitutions Americaine* was published in two volumes. One letter, called "Locke, Milton, and Hume," discusses with quotations the ideas in *The Ready and Easy Way*, and other letters make significant reference to Milton, including "The Right Constitution of a Commonwealth, examined," which employs Milton's beliefs and sense of republicanism. Adams's tract first apeared in 1788.

What these two works by Mirabeau and Salaville lay out for the intellectual and politically minded in France are the arguments we know well against autocratic authority, nonrepresentation in government, a lack of voice in intellectual and social life; and Mirabeau's remarks recount Milton's republican attitudes and works. But the groundwork had been set out earlier. I think of the two 1746 editions into French of Milton's *Treatise on Education*, which emphasizes the precept that Étienne Bonnot de Condillac is credited with," proceeding rigorously from the known to the unknown," and of

Rousseau's *Emile, ou de l'Education* (1762), with its remarks in book 5 on Milton's educational theories. But especially I think of the controversy Voltaire started in 1727 when he added to his *Essay upon the Civil Wars of France* a long discussion aiming at rousing the French poets into major accomplishment, entitled *Essay on the Epick Poetry of the European Nations from Homer down to Milton.* It first appeared in English, but was immediately translated into French. The French journals, like *Bibliothèque Françoise, ou histoire litteraire de la France* and *Journal des scavans,* bristled, and continued to do so years later. Here was negative comparison with that country across the channel, here was a rallying cry for nationalism. Voltaire's own attempt at epic in 1728, *La Henriade,* which exhibits influence from *Paradise Lost* in various ways, brought much vilification, but it was often reprinted. All of the review articles discussed Milton, though primarily in literary terms and with literary criticism at the fore.

Yet Milton and his poem kept being connected with these other issues in France—government, society, justice. Claude Adrien Helvetius, the important philosopher whose ideas colored much political thought during the century, for example, wrote to Montesquieu who was then president of the Bordeaux parliament:

> I have perused . . . the manuscript which you communicated to me [*L'Ésprit des Lois*]. . . . I know nothing that resembles it: indeed I know not whether our French heads are steady enough to enable us to discern all its great beauties. For my own part, I am enraptured with them: I admire the vast genius which created them, and the depth of research which you must have accomplished in order to collect so much knowledge from the rubbish of those barbarian laws, from which I had believed so little could be derived for the instruction or benefit of mankind. I behold

119

you, like the hero of Milton, after having traversed the immensity of chaos, rising illustrious out of darkness.[12]

Of course, the assignment of Satan as hero of *Paradise Lost* long preceded Godwin, Shelley, and Blake. One such thinker, as I have pointed out elsewhere, was Charles Batteux in his analysis of belles-lettres in midcentury, soon translated into English.[13] But beneath this assignment is that admiration for the downtrodden rising up against a seeming tyrant, the thought that the horror of life can be transcended and one can "rise illustrious out of darkness." The cause of Satan was also interestingly juxtaposed in the Colonies to supply material for the revolution of the Americans against George III, such as Philip Freneau and Hugh Henry Brackenridge's *A Poem, on the Rising Glory of America; Being an Exercise Delivered at the Public Commencement at Nassau-Hall, September 25, 1771.*

Yet according to Jean Gillet in a long discussion of "Le Paradis Perdu et l'Ideologie Contre-Revolutionnaire," the epic seems to have been forgotten during the revolution. He asserts that "People no longer showed the least sympathy for the political activity of Milton. The attitude of Mosneron is in this regard exemplary: in 1788, he produced a cautious encomium on the poet's civicism and his relish for liberty. In 1804, he severly censured the seditious Milton."[14] By "civicism" Mosneron meant the principle of government based upon the rights and duties of the individual. This, of course, goes to the heart of the double view of Milton both in France and in England: such concepts of government and liberty as Milton's had led not only to civicism but, horrifyingly, to a reign of terror, the execution of Charles I and that of Louis XVI, the Cromwellian decade and the extremist actions of Danton and Robespierre and their adherents, and the continuing social and economic declines following the

Ninth Thermidor of 27 July 1794. Only with the destruction of the Directory on 9 November 1799, was a new constitution and consulate effected a month and a half later. In her novel *Desmond* (1792), which mentions Milton, Charlotte Smith aligns Edmund Burke and Sir Robert Filmer, and *The Banished Man* (1794) records her disenchantment with the Revolution. In this, Smith likens the character Du Bosse to the Miltonic Satan, but it is the Satan of the altered, nonheroic view.

Jean-Baptiste Mosneron-De Launay had translated *Paradise Lost*, and one reads his encomium as the idealistic view that others like Mirabeau held of Milton. We need look only at the influence upon Andre Chenier in poems like "Aveugle" ("Blind") or "Sur l'Esprit de Parti" or in Chateaubriand's *Milton et Davenant* (1797) for its continued existence during the revolutionary period by sympathizers with the movement. Yet for Mosneron the results were so devastating as to make Milton culpable, just as he had been to Samuel Johnson. Burke talks very positively of Milton often, but almost always in decidedly literary or aesthetic contexts. The new era punctuated by Mme. de Staël's *De la littérature* (1800) and Chateaubriand's *Essai sur la littérature anglaise* (1801) stressed these same contexts and a religious return to faith in God and humanity as well. Seen now against the destruction of life that had ensued, Satan became a revolutionary not to be admired: "Satan announced his intention to surpass the crimes of the English parricides [note the word] and of Cromwell," Jean-François La Harpe asserted in 1804, "and soon appeared to Danton in a dream in the figure of the Protector."[15] Though Mosneron's and La Harpe's attitudes toward Milton as political influence altered their attitudes toward Milton as poet, it has been instead the admiration and pronouncement of Chateaubriand and *Génie du Christianisme* (1804) that has prevailed.

EIGHT

Milton
in Italy in the
Eighteenth Century

M ost of the slight discussion of John Milton and Italy in the eighteenth century has centered on Voltaire's first suggestion and then claim that Milton saw Giovanni Battista Andreini's drama *L'Adamo* while in Florence in 1638–39 and that he later translated his remembrance of it into what became *Paradise Lost*.[1] Voltaire's 1727 statement basically only records the alleged occasion; the revised version—a version in which Voltaire is noticeably negative about Milton's "faults" in *Paradise Lost*—proposes that through this performance Milton conceived of writing a tragedy on the subject, and that later, indeed, he composed an act and a half of what still later became the epic. It is amusing, yet frightening, the way such speculations catch hold and get repeated—or example, this was repeated by Joseph Spence, Alexander Pope's friend, who wrote to his mother on 2 December 1729 of Milton's use of this source for the poem.[2]

One rejection of Voltaire's whimsical fiction came in Giuseppi Baretti's *A Dissertation upon the Italian Poetry, In which are interspersed some Remarks on Mr. Voltaire's Essay on the Epic Poets* (London, 1753). He quotes Voltaire's account and proceeds to correct its inaccuracies and superficial knowledge, and suggests a more likely source in Dante. "If he had read the life, or even the writings of Milton himself," Baretti comments of Voltaire, "he would have perceived by them that Florence, when that poet traveled through Italy, was full of learned men; and if he had the least notion of the Florentine people, he would have spoken with less contempt of them" (66). He calls Andreini "a mean ridiculous comedian." Much of this is repeated in Baretti's *Discours sur Shakespeare et sur Monsieur de Voltaire* (Paris, 1777).

Nonetheless, William Hayley, in his *Conjectures on the Origin of the Paradise Lost*, which was added to his 1796 *The Life of Milton, in Three Parts*, concluded that "Andreini . . . appears . . . highly worthy of our notice" (250). Hayley reprints extracts from the play. But source-hunting continued, and though without the antagonism of Voltaire, it undermines Milton's originality, even when Hayley discusses Milton's originality. It is amazing that so many of these critics appear to equate anything written on the Adam and Eve story or on the war in heaven with a source for Milton's work, as if he had not read and known the Bible and its commentaries. For Hayley further advances yet another Italian source, Troilo Lancetta's *La Scena Tragica d'Adamo ed Eva* (Venetia, 1644), which an appendix offers in a prose analysis, as well as the *Angeleida* of Erasmo Valvasone (Venetia, 1590). Hayley became aware of Lancetta's play as a result of "a literary curiosity, which my accomplished friend, Mr. Walker, to whom the literature of Ireland has many obligations, very kindly sent me, on his return from an excursion to Italy, where it happened to strike a traveler, whose mind is peculiarly awakened to elegant pursuits" (264).[3]

This Mr. Walker was Joseph Cooper Walker, who discussed all these works in his own *Historical Memoir on Italian Tragedy, From the Earliest Period to the Present Times* (London, 1799). Hayley proposed Valvasone as a source because the poem "consists of three cantos on the War of Heaven, and is singularly terminated by a sonnet, addressed to the triumphant Archangel Michael" (271). Section 2 of Walker's study, pp. 160–73, reviews the alleged relationships of *Paradise Lost* and these three authors, with quotations in Italian and English. Reference is again made in Walker's Appendix I (vi–vii) and Appendix VI (xxxii–xxxvi) is entitled, "Thoughts on the Origin of Milton's Paradise Lost." To the foregoing suggestions, Walker added Giambattista Marino's "Gerusalemme Distrutta." Appendix IX (xlix–xlvii) presents a passage from Andreini's *L'Adamo*, and Appendix X (xlviii–lvi), the prose analysis of Lancetta's piece, both taken from Hayley's *Conjectures*. (Since Walker's work seems not to have found its way into Milton scholarship, perhaps I should note that there are numerous citations and comments throughout the study, including, for example, the suggestion that the "Hail Wedded Love" apostrophe in book 4 derived from Milton's reading of an anonymous "Dialogo del modo di tor moglie," pp. 91–92; and that the Morning Hymn of book 5 is similar to the opening of Antonio Decio da Horte's "Acripanda," p. 112. Milton's visit to Rome and his alleged introduction to Pope Urban VIII, p. 144 n., and "An Attempt to ascertain the Site of the Villa near Naples, in which the Marquis Manso received Tasso and Milton. With Notices of the Manso Family," pp. xxvi–xxxi [Appendix V], are also reviewed. In addition, Walker refers to a partial translation of *Paradise Lost* by Antonio Conti [p. 229], and cites approvingly Oliver Goldsmith's comment that Scipione

Maffei knew and employed *Samson Agonistes* [p. 233 n.][4] Reference is to Maffei's five-act tragedy *La Merope*, which has a dedicatory preface discussing tragedy and epic poems, dated 1713. But neither the preface nor the play itself seems to me to reflect Milton's "Of a Dramatic Poem" or *Samson Agonistes*.)

But there is much more than the claim of Italian sources for the epic to establish Milton's strong and positive reputation in Italy in the eighteenth century. Aside from the Conti translation just mentioned, an unpublished poetic version from 1715–16, translations were made by Lorenzo Magalotti of the first 241 lines of book 1 (to be found in a manuscript in the British Library); by Antonio Salvini ca. 1721 (to be found in manuscript in the Biblioteca Riccardiana); the wedding hymn by Francesco Gherardelli in 1787; the "Prospetto del Paradiso Perduto," that is, a synopsis of the poem, translated into "versi sciolti" (blank verse) by Alessandro Ercole Pepoli in 1795. Paolo Antonio Rolli founded his *Sabrina, a Masque*, in three acts, on Milton's *A Mask* in 1737; the edition gives both the Italian and the English. Let it be noted that this dramatic poetic version was published before John Dalton's famous adaptation was even performed in 1738, after which Milton's *A Mask* has always been called *Comus*—illogical though that may be. Thomas Arne's music for Dalton's theatrical piece was immediately published by I. Walsh, but so were *The Favourite Songs in the Opera call'd Sabrina* immediately published by Walsh after its first performance. In addition, Giuseppe Lavini produced "Il Paradiso riaguistato opposto ad Paradiso perduto," in 1750–56 and Domenico Testa published "L'Allegro" in 1785.

But the two important Italian translations of the major epic were by Rolli in 1729–35 and by Felice Mariottini in 1794–96. Rolli's 1729 verse translation of books 1–6 was accompanied by a life that included various shorter poems and the testimonials from Milton's Italian friends published with the Latin poems in 1645. The important second edition from Verona in 1730 included "osservazioni Sopra il Libro del Signor Voltaire che esamina l'Epica Poesia delle Nazioni Europee," in which Rolli takes Voltaire to task for his absurd thesis. The translation of the full poem appeared from the Press of Carlo Bennet in 1735, and was frequently reprinted from various presses and places during the century, right up through 1794. In 1750 the Italian translation of Joseph Addison's *annotazioni sopra tutto il Poema* was added, and these observations and the critique continued to be part of the ensuing publication of Rolli's well-known translation. Indeed, it had been so well known immediately through its 1730 printing that the Roman Catholic Camera Apostolica placed it on the Index of prohibited books on 21 January 1732.

Mariottini published a new translation of book 1 in Italian unrhymed verse in 1794 from the press of P. Molini; the second edition was from the press of G. Polidori in 1796. Arguments in Italian prose were included; Rolli had given two-to-four line verse summaries. The 1794 edition presents the English text as footnotes to the Italian, although not in synchronized lines as one of the reviews notes, and a long preface often criticizing Samuel Johnson and his discussion of Milton and his works. It also included Newton's Life and Addison's critique, and was to be completed in five volumes. The full text of the poem presented in 1796 is in two volumes, with a brief preface and no Life or critique. There is a notice in The *Monthly Review* for the 1794 edition, and *The Critical Review* got around to printing its comments only in 1796.[5] The reviewer for this journal found the translation "rather diffuse" though it "seems . . . in general faithful."

Mariottini had negative things to say about Milton's Italian poems in the Preface, and the reviewer remarks on this in a seemingly objective fashion, but we can discern his lack of agreement with that judgment.

Prior to this time, however, another review had appeared in the February 1794 issue of *The British Critic*,[6] which called forth a 36-page rebuttal entitled, *An Italian Warning to the British Critic, or an Elucidation of the British Critic's Review of Mariottini's Translation of Paradise Lost* (1794). The discussion in *The British Critic* was reprinted, and a section-by-section "elucidation" was given in defense of the translation. The reviewer in the *Critic* had discussed blank verse, but apparently from a prejudged position of unhappiness with blank verse, a not uncommon position from 1667 onward. (We remember that Milton added the statement "The Verse" in the second issue of 1668, clearly in argument with a position encased in John Dryden's *Essay of Dramatick Poesie* of 1668.) The critic writes: "ordinary blank verse is written with ease from the simplicity of its rules, but excellent poems are much more rarely produced, when attempted in that measure, than in any other" (173). The critic states of Milton's Italian verse that Baretti had commended it to Johnson and that he selected it as a flower of Italian composition; the Italian warning counters: "it is certain that Italy never had any particular esteem for Baretti" (16). Mariottini's disagreement with Johnson on the worth of Antonio Francini's testimonial helped label Johnson the Aretino of British literature. The critic was incensed. He demonstrates faults that he finds in the translation—like amplification into nonpoetic treatment—but he also concludes that the translator "thoroughly informed with the poet's spirit, and glowing from the effect of his harmonious numbers, . . . faithfully and majestically gives us the *soul* and *body* of the poet together" (176).

The full translation brought a notice in *The Monthly Magazine* 1 (1796): 407, as "Milton's *Paradise Lost*, translated into Italian Blank Verse, by Felix Marionni." *The Critical Review* gave a brief review to the full poem in volume 20 (July 1797): 343; and *The British Critic*, perhaps somewhat chastened, offered comparative quotations of Milton, Rolli, and Mariottini, with generally positive remarks, in article 10 of its volume 10 for 1797, pp. 519–21.

It should be clear that the literati of Italy in the eighteenth century were aware of Milton as poet, primarily of *Paradise Lost*, but also as a poetic force. And one should also note the long subscriber list of Mariottini's 1794 volume. Conti discussed *Paradise Lost*, its erudition and sublimity, its epic status and comparison with other works, its characters, religious import, setting, and pictures, in statements on Italian poetry, as well as in a letter (in French) to Mme. la Présidente Ferraut, dated 13 August 1719.[7] The first edition of Johann Jacob Bodmer's German prose translation, *Verlust des Paradieses. Ein Helden-Gedicht*, appeared in 1732, but he and Pietro Calepio had been discussing the poem and the translation in letters written in the years before. These letters, now in the Biblioteca Curia di Bergamo, dated in 1729–30, are concerned with meaning in the poem and adequate reproduction of that meaning in translation. Salvini referred to Milton's Italian verses in 1733,[8] and Baretti noticed Milton and his poem in *The Italian Library. Containing An Account of the Lives and Works of the Most Valuable authors of Italy* (London, 1757), p. 140.

A Spanish poet and critic in Italy, Juan Andrès, published in his important six-volume *Dell'Origine, De' Progressi e Dello Stato Attuale D'Ogni Letteratura dell'abate D. Giovanni Andres* in Venice in 1783–87. In it he discusses Milton's sublimity, *Paradise Lost* and its influence, as well as epic and tragedy in general of which

Paradise Lost is a prime example and *Comus, Paradise Lost*, and *Samson Agonistes* as musical pieces (opera and oratorio). Further, Count Magalotti wrote to Lord Somers on July 1709, concerning Milton and *Paradise Lost*, and John Philips and Magalotti's translation of *Cyder* (*Il Sidro*, published in 1749).[9] (Somers is often credited with bringing into being the 1688 fourth edition of *Paradise Lost*, with its illustrations largely by Sir John Baptista de Medina.) Salvino Salvini discussed Carlo Dati and Milton in 1717,[10] and Count Francesco Algarotti alluded to Milton and his works in letters to Francesco Maria Zanotti, dated 13 November 1754; to Vicenzo Corrazza, dated 28 December 1755; to Marchese Pirieto Malvezzi, dated 19 September 1757; and elsewhere.[11] Algarotti's translation of Addison and Steele's *The Spectator, The Tatler*, and *The Guardian* (published in 1753 in Livorno) should also be noted, for here there are comments by the translator as well as quotation in Italian of portions of *Paradise Lost*; for example, the Morning Hymn from Rolli's translation is quoted in *Speculazione LXXI*.[12]

Another critical problem for later times was the publication of *La Tina Equivoci Rusticali in cinquanta Sonetti di Antonio Malatesti Fiorentino* in 1757. Another edition is undated.[13] We are told that in September 1637 Malatesti composed these sonnets and that they were given to Milton, supposedly when he was in Florence in August–September 1638 or in April 1639, but perhaps modern scholarship should cast a doubtful eye on the actuality of this event. The edition includes other remarks sent to Thomas Brand by Giovanni Lami ([3]–7). Brand is supposed to have discovered the manuscript sometime before 1757 in a London bookshop, then giving it to his friend Thomas Hollis, who sent a copy of it on 2 June 1761 to the Della Crusca Academy in Florence,[14] of which Malatesti had been a member and where Milton apparently read some of his Latin verse. This manuscript or a copy was sold at Sotheby's in 1817. A translation of the prefatory epistle "Nencio alla Tina" and of the sonnets by Donald Sears is published in *Milton Studies* 13 (1979): 275–317. One does wonder what Milton made of all the sexual double entendre in the poems, if indeed Malatesti presented the poems to him. Sears makes some reasonable connections with such punning in Milton's attacks on Alexander More in 1654 and 1655, and concludes, "If my conjectures are correct, Milton the linguist and humanist was less shocked than Masson's traditional interpretation supposes" (281).

Clear indications of the status of Milton in Italian literature of the eighteenth century are the frequent discussions in Carlo Denina's *Discorso sopra le vicende della Letterature* (Torino, 1761). Particularly significant are the recountings of Voltaire's charge concerning Andreini's *L'Adamo*, of the Lauder affair, of Voltaire's and Louis Racine's difficulties in appreciating and accepting the allegory of Sin and Death, of Milton's preference for *Paradise Regain'd*, and Denina's summary of Milton's biography and the contrast between his poetic achievement and his governmental work for Cromwell and against Charles I.

Milton in Italy in the eighteenth century, however, has another side, one unnoticed before: the significance of Milton and his work for English poets living and writing in Italy. We are all aware that a number of the Romantic poets—like Shelley and Keats and Byron—offer numerous examples of Miltonic influence even in poems of Italian context, like Shelley's "Lines Written Among the Euganean Hills" or Byron's "Stanzas Written on the Road Between Florence and Pisa," which should be read with "Lycidas" firmly in our minds, for it seems clearly to have been in Byron's thoughts. But before any of the three were even born, a not dissimilar colony was producing poetry in Italy that should not be labeled "pre-Romantic" but rather "Romantic" as we have come to use that term. One member of that colony, who seems totally forgotten by students of the eighteenth and nineteenth centuries alike, William Parsons, flourished around 1785 and died in 1807. The prejudices against Romantic poetry are manifest in Thomas Seccombe's account of Parsons in the *Dictionary of National Biography*, when he talks of Parsons's "puerilities" and "trivialities . . . eked out by imitations, translations, and complimentary verses." To Seccombe (1866–1923), assistant editor of the *DNB*, and professor of English at Sandhurst and in the last years of his life at Queen's University in Kingston, Ontario, Parsons's poems were "effusions." Seccombe, we might snidely note, could boast only a B. A. from Balliol.

The Arcadian Academy in Rome on the Janiculum, but called the Serbatoio, was founded in 1690 and continued existence until 1800. Among its members were Paolo Rolli, for instance, and also Parsons, who resided in the mid-1780s in Florence. (He was elected to the Royal Society in England in 1787). But the hub for the expatriot literati was Florence. The group of English writers centered there published *The Florence Miscellany* from the press of G. Cam (that is, Gaetano Cambiagi) in Florence in 1785. Aside from Parsons's work, it included poems by Bertie Greatheed; Hester Lynch Thrale Piozzi, Samuel Johnson's friend, who married Gabriel Piozzi on 23 July 1784 (and again two days later); and Robert Merry, who wrote under the pseudonym of Della Crusca.

Mrs. Piozzi's diary for the 1780s has numerous allusions to or quotations from Milton's works.[15] The poetic endeavors of the collection do more than Mrs. Thrale, in her preface, says: "Why we wrote the verses may be easily explain'd, we wrote them to divert ourselves, and to say kind things of each other." While Parsons's "To Mrs. Piozzi In Reply Written on the Anniversary of Her Wedding 25 July 1785" may say kind things about her and her husband who had joined the group, it attempts to achieve a resonance in lines like "Sooth'd by soft Musick's seducing delights" with its play of sibilants, not very far from those Shelleyan "To Music" poems. And the not very usual word "reciprocal" in the line "And best with reciprocal love" suggests an iamb and two anapests, creating rhythm not very commonplace for the eighteenth century. (The poem will also be found in John Debrett's *An Asylum for Fugitive Pieces* in 1786.) The group first met at a Mr. Meghitt's pensione, then later at a different hotel, after which such Italians as Count Angelo d'Elci and the Marquis Ippolito Pindemonte joined them. There had been political/literary reasons for their existence, and there were political/literary arguments that eventually caused disruption in friendship, not unlike events some 35 years later.

Robert Merry adapted the name Della Crusca in a kind of defiance by 29 June 1787, his first use of it in print. He had gone to Italy in 1784 because of the oppression of Italian nationalism, and Grand Duke Leopold had abolished the Accademia della Crusca in Florence on 7 July 1783 because of its championing of Italian freedom through its literary activities. Leopold established in replacement the Accademia Fiorentina, which Merry joined, along with others, in an effort to reestablish the political integrity of Italian letters. *The Florence Miscellany* of 1785 attests to the unmuzzling of that Italian muse, as Mrs. Thrale puts it. Just earlier after he had arrived, Merry produced *The Arno Miscellany Being a Collection of Fugitive Pieces Written by the Members of a Society called the Oziosi at Florence*, published in Florence in 1784. The whole is a put-on with such items as "Exultation. A Pastoral Translated from the Original Babelonian By

M. R." with its "pensive Oak" and "silvan coolness," and this is followed by "Cruddroddruck. An Ode Translated from the Celtic by Mr. M. . . . After seeing the foregoing Pastoral." (The latter is a Pindaric and dated 2 March 1784). In 1789 Merry and Greatheed became violent partisans for the French Revolution through their sense of the oppression of the French people, not different much in attitudes of justice from Wordsworth or the later Byron or Shelley, but blind to the problems that Burke saw. Merry broke with Greatheed and Parsons later, ostensibly over his courting and championing of Anna Matilda (that is, Hannah Cowley, who was married, though her marriage was unknown at this time to Merry). However, a holograph letter dated 29 April 1788 in the John Rylands Library makes clear that other reasons involved envy and literary causes.

Merry's *Paulina; or, The Russian Daughter, a Poem. In two Books. By Robert Merry, Esq. Member of the Royal Academy of Florence, Late La Crusca* (London, 1787) employs Miltonic language and diction throughout, and appropriates *Comus*, 47, in the poem (p. 17 and n.). The title page describes Merry as "Member of the Royal Academy of Florence, Late La Crusca," with its political jibe. Interest in things somewhat remote from ordinary life, in the somewhat exotic, in the twists romance may take, in the horrific aspects of killing and death, the poem tells the story of a girl whose lover is murdered, who is sexually assaulted and who then slays the evil one. She enters a convent in atonement. Though written in heroic couplets, the poem employs language that breaks with much eighteenth century verse and looks forward to poetry some 15 to 35 years later:

> Inspire my sorr'wing verse, which strives to show
> The start of anguish, and the shriek of woe,
> The pray'r half utter'd, and the tear half shed,

When first Paulina found her lover dead.
For ruthless fate had seal'd th'eternal doom,
And changed his place of refuge to a tomb . . .
O night accurst, when vice exulting reign'd,
And virtue sunk, and innocence was stain'd!

Mrs. Thrale's epitome of the poem was "a prodigious Series of beautiful Lines, & nobody looks even at That" (diary entry of 21 May 1787).

Two of Merry's contributions to *The Florence Miscellany* were influenced by Milton's companion poems—"Il Vaggio" (that is, the wanderer) and "La Dimora" (that is, the homebody)—but they turn on romantic content quite different from something like William Mason's "Il Pacifico" and "Il Bellicoso," written a couple of decades before. In "Il Vaggio," pp. 196–202, Merry draws on "L'Allegro" for his first ten lines and for octosyllabics, and in "La Dimora," pp. 203–08, drawn from "Il Penseroso," he alludes to Milton directly. In the same year and from the same press as the *Miscellany* appeared a volume of verse by Merry (using a pseudonym) supposedly translated from the Italian, with Italian and English facing texts, *Roberto Manners Poemetto In Versi Sciolti* (that is, in blank verse). Again there is a championing of liberty and of Italian resistance to political realities, thus the pseudonym and thus the nonstrictured verse. In *Diversity. A Poem. By Della Crusca* (London, 1788), he apostrophizes Milton and his greatness (21–22). He also published *Elegy on the Death of Magdalen Marchioness Corsi*, in English and Italian, with an inscription of 9 October 1785, Florence (apparently being published there at that time).

Another author related to the group (under various pseudonyms) was Mary Robinson, a poet and novelist, whose *Ainsi Va Le Monde, A Poem . . . By Laura Maria* (London, 1790), is inscribed to Merry; there are allusions to Milton in the poem (3, 5). Her *Sappho and Phaon. In a Series of Legitimate Sonnets, with Thoughts on Poetical Subjects, and Anecdotes of the Grecian Princess* (London, 1796) called forth discussion of Milton and his Italian poems and sonnets by the reviewer in *The Monthly Review* 24 (1797): 17.[16]

For *The Florence Miscellany* Greatheed supplied "A Dream," pp. 7–13, with language and images drawn from *Paradise Lost* and an allusion in the poem; and Parson's work includes "Epistle to the Marquis Ippolito Pindemonte at Verona," with an adaptation of *Paradise Lost* 9.1036 (p. 29); "To Mrs. Piozzi In Reply Written on the Anniversary of Her Wedding 25 July 1785," replete with Miltonic language (p. 45); "Ode to Sleep Written at Midnight," which imitates "Il Penseroso" (pp. 65–67); "Sonnetto del Conte Angelo d'Elci Cavaliere di Malta," in Italian, with an allusion in the poem (p. 123 and n.); "On the Pleasures of Poetry," with an allusion and an adaptation of "Arcades," 73–74 (p. 135 and n.); and "Vallombrosa" (pp. 173–87), but without an epigraph. "On the Pleasures of Poetry" was also printed in *The European Magazine* 9 (1786): 365. Parsons's verse is often in truncated octosyllabics, the meter of Milton's companion poems, or in rhymed couplets, as well as sonnets and odes.

All these poems and others of pertinency were published in his *A Poetical Tour, in the Years 1784, 1785, and 1786. By a member of the Arcadian Society at Rome* (London, 1787). Other poems by Parsons to be noted in this collection are "Ode to Variety, written at Bath," with an allusion in the poem and quotation of *Paradise Lost* 4.247 (p. 4 and n.); "Ode to the Lake of Geneva," with its reference and remembrance of *Paradise Lost* 4.224–25 ("Through the shaggy hill/Pass'd underneath ingulf'd"; p. 24 n.); "To the Marquis Ippolito Pindemonte, Noble Venetian, On his Poem on the defence of Gibralter, entitled 'Gibilterra Salvata'," with an allusion in the poem (p. 39); "Song" with an adaptation of the last line of "Canzone" (p. 60 and n.); the epigraph from *Paradise Lost* 1.302–04, added to "Vallombrosa" (p. 84); "Ode on Visiting the Site of Horace's Sabine Villa," with adaptation of "L'Allegro," 151–52 (p. 115 and n.); and "Epistle from Naples, to Bertie Greethead [sic]," with a quotation of *Comus*, 520, and adaptations of *Comus*, 882, *Paradise Lost* 11.746–47, and *Paradise Lost* 5.282–83 (pp. 140 n., 146 and n., 151 and nn.). Parsons later published *An Ode to A Boy at Eton, with Three Sonnets, and One Epigram* (London, 1796) and *Fidelity, or, Love at First Sight. A Tale. With other Poems* (London, 1798). The Boy at Eton is Great-heed, and various poems in the collection quote, adapt, or are influenced by "Il Penseroso," *Paradise Lost*, and "On Shakespear." The latter collection indicates the continuing influence of "Il Penseroso" and *Paradise Lost*, and also of the sonnets. Further, Parsons published *Elegy Written at Florence* (Geneva, 1785) and *Odes* (Rome, 1786), which are included in *A Poetical Tour*.

Perhaps we can stress as earmarks of romanticism—impossible though definition is—freedom from the restraints and rules of classicism, an individualism dominated by imagination with an emphasis on nature and emotion, and with the individual as center. Parsons is not a great poet, but he is better, all prejudices against the Romantics aside, than he has been accounted. He is more on the level of Samuel Rogers, who also reflects a study of Milton and whose poem *Italy* was written in 1819–34.

Parsons's "Epistle from Naples," written around 1786 and published the next year, exemplifies this description of "romantic," and one might think of the clearly superior but in many ways similar poem, Shelley's "Stanzas Written in Dejection, Near Naples," 1818. His "Vallombrosa" is obviously linked with *Paradise Lost*, but its octosyllabic couplets link it as well with "L'Allegro" and that poem's celebration of nature. (I give excerpts from both poems in the notes section since they are not readily available to readers.[17])

I would point out that the poems to which I have referred might very easily have been the kind of contemporary verse that the 15-year-old or so Wordsworth and the 13-year-old or so Coleridge would have been reading in their schoolboy days. One of Wordsworth's endeavors in 1786, "Composed in Anticipation of Leaving School," is appropriate enough for comparison. As with Parsons's work, the poem is strongly influenced by Milton, here specifically by the ending of "Lycidas":

> Dear native regions, I foretell,
> From what I feel at this farewell,
> That, wheresoe'er my steps may tend,
> And whensoe'er my course shall end,
> If in that hour a single tie
> Survive of local sympathy,
> My soul will cast the backward view,
> The longing look alone on you.
>
> Thus, while the sun sinks down to rest
> Far in the regions of the west,
> Though to the vale no parting beam
> Be given, not one memorial gleam,
> A lingering light he fondly throws
> On the dear hills where first he rose.

Milton's presence in Italy in the eighteenth century is noticeably more than most people would probably have guessed, as evidenced by editions, criticism, imitation, and the affinity some English poets sensed and employed to their own advantage. One could almost fantasize that it was Milton who prepared the way for the British poetic love of Italy in the eighteenth and nineteenth centuries, and counseled their inspiration at every turn. It is no wonder that John Langhorne capitalized upon such presence by translating Milton's Italian poems and addressing them "To a Gentleman of Italy" (apparently Signor Marco Antonio de' Mozzi of Florence) in 1776, or that in 1740 the companion poems—as Italian texts, adapted by Charles Jennens, to which a third part, "Il Moderato," was added — were set to music by George Frederick Händel. The musical production—actually a truly English work— became one of the most popular of pieces during the century, a fact to be explained by Händel's popularity, the interest in Italian opera, Milton's popularity, and, I am sure, the exotic aura of "il fior novo di strania favella."

NINE

The American Milton: Imitation, Creative Spirit, and Presence

A nineteenth century American editor of John Milton's works, R. W. Griswold, observed in 1845 that "Milton is more emphatically *American* than any author who has lived in the United States."[1] The connotations of that adjective *American* are numerous, and one's understanding of the remark is undoubtedly dependent upon one's prejudices. Griswold's intentionality in the sentence may also be debated. But he does seem to be pointing out that those ideas and attitudes that had become associated with the word "American" in political, social, and literary thinking are exemplified by Milton and his works more clearly, forcefully, and sustainedly than in the works of some authors born and raised in the United States. Among those ideas and attitudes, Griswold may have been thinking of the power of the demos, whether politically, religiously, or sociologically, a demos that is not stratified by society and thus not by economics and politics and religion—or at least not theoretically. Part of that nonstratification extends to gender, although Griswold probably did not think of that and probably would not have acceded to it as viable. However, Milton's works—if we take all of them over the full range of his career—do reveal an awareness of differences among people, first, on the basis of intellectual ability, and second, on the related bases of education, "right reason," and culture.

A continuing aim of Milton's life and works was to minimize the significance of those intellectual differences through education and what should be education's resultant ideas and attitudes, although the continuance of intellectual differences be biological. As to gender differences, his work manifests his belief that they may be made less and less important, and he exalts women to superior position, even though he accepts throughout a biblical—largely Pauline—concept of male over female. He did not, nor could he with his religious background, I suppose, recognize that the Bible was written by men, who lived in a Hebraic social world in which woman was held to be only helpmate and thus inferior. This position for woman has not changed today for orthodox sects, any more than it has for many Christian groups. What Milton affirms is a subordinationist belief similar to that in theological matters where God the Father is superior to God the Son and both to God the Holy Spirit, but all together constitute the triune God. So male is superior to female, but together they constitute Humankind as a duality.

Part of what may lie behind Griswold's remark is also his argument with Sir Egerton Brydges, an English editor of Milton's poetical works and biographer in 1835 (and later). Brydges divorced the poet Milton from the political writer Milton, and thereby condemned ideas of kingship and republicanism found in such works as *The Tenure of*

Kings and Magistrates, the *First Defense of the English People,* and *Eikonoklastes.* This dichotomy was not only Samuel Johnson's, but Joseph Addison's in "An Account of the Greatest English Poets," from 1694, and Thomas Yalden's, in reaction to the 1698 reprinting of all of the prose works. For Milton argues against monarchy when that monarchy does not discharge its duties toward the people it is supposed to represent and lead. And since, prior to 1649, Charles I had been the figurehead of that monarchy, eliciting sympathy from the people by his alleged meditations when he was in prison through the "king's book," *Eikon Basilike,* Milton's attack on the falsity of that work and Charles's hypocrisy brought vilification upon Milton's head. *The Tenure* was written in January 1649 when Charles was being tried for his crimes against the people by the Parliamentarians. The trial ended with condemnation and execution by beheading. Milton, since he became the Secretary for Foreign Tongues to the Council of State, was thus associated in people's minds with the regicides. He does not argue *for* regicide in *The Tenure,* but he does argue that the power of kings and magistrates has been conferred upon them by the people in covenant for common peace and benefit; when their power is abused, it is the people's right and duty to reassume that power or to alter it in whatever way is most conducive to public good. The people's natural rights as God's creatures predicate this conception of the social contract. Following Calvinist principle, Milton contends that popular resistance to royal or civil authority is lawful when executed by magistrates properly charged with responsibility or when the person's divinely free conscience is repressed by secular action. It sounds very much like the thinking of the founding fathers of the United States, and in fact it is.

Milton conceived of his task in *The Tenure* to set down how kings came into being, their responsibilites, the nature of tyranny, and the duty of the people to depose and punish the tyrant legally. He does not concern himself with judging or sentencing Charles. However, since rumors were rife foretelling the denunication and execution of Charles, Milton does refer to the matter, but all he says is that the Presbyterians, by their deceitful acts, have virtually killed the king and that putting a king to death after due conviction and deposition may be necessary. One may conclude that Milton's critics have not read the works; they are simply repeating a denouncement that has become a cliché.

Specifically, Brydges had disputed Milton's denial of the divine right of kings, which the Stuart monarchs had claimed. Milton wrote, "to say Kings are accountable to none but God, is the overturning of all Law and government," which goes to the heart of the defense for Charles, whose execution is looked upon by the people as a sacrilege against God. Charles had been likened to David the King, that is, the Son in his kingly role, and *Eikon Basilike* played upon Charles's being a figure of Christ, both in language and in the title page illustration. But as we know, the king's book was written, not by Charles, but by his chaplain John Gauden with the assistance of Bishop Brian Duppa. Nonetheless, in Brydges's day Christopher Wordsworth produced *Who Wrote Eikon Basilike? Considered and Answered, in Two Letters, Addressed to His Grace the Archbishop of Canterbury* (1824), deciding that indeed it was Charles.

I cite this material to try to describe the American Milton. It is clear from what has been said that Milton's ideas, more than a century before the American Revolution and the formation of a new government, lie intertextually with the concepts of rebellion against those who usurp the people's natural birthright of government and religion: "a King for crimes proportionall," Milton wrote, "should forfet all his title and inheritance to the people: unless the people must be thought created all for him, he not for them, and they all in one body inferior to him single, which were a kinde of treason against the dignity of mankind to affirm." The difference that Thomas Hobbes was to offer was the thought that as long as the people gave up their personal action to a king for protection and leadership, then they have no recourse against that king later on.

Hobbes, of course, in many ways was important to the eighteenth century development of governmental and constitutional issues, but in this and some other ways the other two important writers from this period for the American revolutionists were followers of Milton. The first, John Locke, specifically attacked Hobbes in his *Two Treatises of Government,* and his *Letter Concerning Toleration* comes straight out of Milton's tracts, especially *Of True Religion, Hæresie, Schism, Toleration,* which is so meaningful for the separation of church and state. Locke writes, for instance, "The one only narrow way which leads to heaven is not better known to the magistrate than to private persons, and therefore I cannot safely take him for my guide, who may probably be as ignorant of the way as myself, and who certainly is less concerned for my salvation than I myself am." Locke, as we know from his manuscripts, read carefully such works as *Of Reformation, The Doctrine and Discipline of Divorce, Areopagitica, The Tenure, Paradise Lost,* the 1698 *Complete Collection* of the prose, the *First Defence,* and *Eikonoklastes.*

The other important author was Algernon Sidney, who was beheaded for his views and for "treason" in 1683. *The Very Copy of a Paper Delivered to the Sheriffs, Upon the Scaffold on Tower-Hill, on Friday, Decemb. 7. 1683. By Algernon Sidney, Esq; Before His Execution There* employed sentences taken directly from *The Tenure* in defense of himself and his ideas. His *Discourses Concerning Government*, drawn from the *First Defence* and *The Tenure*, with specific reference to and quotation from book 9 of *Paradise Lost*, was printed and reprinted throughout the eighteenth century. Antagonists to the republican movements in England and America repeatedly chalk up the rising issues against the established government to Locke and Sidney, whose works are repeatedly republished, and Milton is sometimes included with them.

As we move to the period of the American Revolution, we find that it is Milton who is most cited and quoted in manuscripts, letters, and some printed works by John Adams and Benjamin Franklin and Thomas Jefferson. And of course it is Thomas Paine's *Common Sense* in 1776 that is so instrumental in the action of the times and so frequently reprinted, and there we find a quotation from *Paradise Lost* as epitomizing the impossibility of reconcilement between two such opposed forces as the government of England and the aggrieved former colonists in America. But perhaps fewer people know Adams's very important and often reprinted *Thoughts on Government: Applicable to the Present State of the American Colonies* printed in early 1776, in which Adams discusses Milton's republicanism and the divorce sonnet, "I did but prompt the age to quit thir clogs," and shows strong influence from *The Ready and Easy Way to Establish A Free Commonwealth*. The papers of Thomas Jefferson, dated from 1776 through 1791, yield extensive notes from *Of Reformation* and *Of Prelatical Episcopacy, Reason of Church-Government* and *An Apology for Smectymnuus*, and of course various sections of *Paradise Lost*.

It is indeed *Paradise Lost* that supplies so much of the substance of the epical poems in the early days of the United States, though Miltonists may not be especially happy with the employment of Satan's rebellion against God as supplying material for the revolution of the Americans against George III. Among the earliest examples is Philip Freneau and Hugh Henry Brackenridge's *A Poem, on the Rising Glory of America; Being an Exercise Delivered at the Public Commencement at Nassau-Hall, September 25, 1771*, where the influence from *Paradise Lost* has been recognized in language, content, tone, and the use of blank verse, but the employment of *On the Morning of Christ's Nativity* has not generally been noticed. And we all may be aware of Joel Barlow's dependence on Milton's epic in *The Vision of Columbus* (1787) and its revision, *The Columbiad* (1807). But two little known works by a Scotsman who traveled to this country celebrate American victories shortly before new government had been effected, and these come right out of the same kind of Miltonic imitation; I refer to Richard Colvill's *Atalanta* (that is, Atlanta) in 1773 and *Savannah* in 1780. Another well-known poem dealing with liberty and assertions against monarchic presumptions is *Cow-Chace, In Three Cantos, Published on Occasion of the Rebel General Wayne's Attack of the Refugees Block-House on Hudson's River, on Friday the 21st of July, 1780.* To this, in the New York edition by James Rivington, was added Camillo Querno's (that is, apparently, Jonathan Odell's) *The American Times, a Satire, in Three Parts. In which are delineated the characters of the American Rebellion.* A contrast on the side of the rebels will be found in Peter Markoe's *The Times* (1788). All are obviously and clearly Miltonic in content and in poetic technique.

In other epics, Satan and his cohorts supply both invalidity of revolt against the true leader and validation of the need to revolt when the monarch has become oppressive. The view of Satan in these numerous poems—like the anonymous *Fredoniad*, for example—preludes the view of Satan usually assigned to the English Romantics. Satan becomes equated with Prometheus for some, and injustice toward the people is stressed. *Paradise Lost* supplies the subtext.

I have moved from the American Milton as influence on political thinking to an American Milton as influence in justifications and criticisms of the American Revolution. The influence of Milton, particularly of *Paradise Lost*, is ubiquitous in the eighteenth century for poetic achievement as well, and this defines a different sense for the term American Milton. We remember Timothy Dwight's works, for instance, like *The Conquest of Canaan* or *Greenfield Hill*. We may not be aware of his *The Triumph of Infidelity: A Poem* (1788), which has a section in which he talks about Milton's blindness. We may not be aware of Philip Freneau's parodic comments in *Tracts and Essays on Several Subjects*, talking of the City Poet, in 1788. Here some of the traits of inept Miltonic imitators, whose name is legion, are ridiculed.

We know of William Livingston, governor of New Jersey, and David Humphreys, one of Washington's colonels (and later one of the Hartford wits), but we may be less aware of their Miltonic poems, like *Philosophic Solitude* and *America* by Livingston, or *Address to America* and *A Poem, On the Happiness of America; Addressed to the Citizens of the United States*, by Humphreys. The American Milton is a strong presence, as we can see in prose like Adams's *A Defence of the Constitutions of Government of the United States of America* (1788), where one should look at Letter 55, entitled, "Locke, Milton, and Hume," with its quotation and discussion of the ideas of *The Ready and Easy Way*, and also the total revision of that book in the same year, where in Letter 6 Adams discusses "The Right Constitution of a Commonwealth, examined," employing Milton's ideas and sense of republicanism. A poem not published until 1856 but completed before 1788, Richard Alsop's *The Charms of Fancy. A Poem. In Four Cantos*, demonstrates well the pull of Milton's language and diction in *Paradise Lost*, but perhaps also the fourfold structure of *Paradise Regain'd* which was to come to dominate the work of the English Romantics.

But this kind of presence is seen too by quotation and some discussion, particularly noteworthy, I think, when it appears in periodicals and in kinds of writing other than poems. *The American Museum, or Repository of Ancient and Modern Fugitive Pieces*, for example, prints "An Oration in Praise of Ignorance. Delivered at the Commencement in the University of Pennsylvania, July 4, 1781; being the Anniversary of the Declaration of Independence." The unknown author knew Milton's seventh prolusion on "Learning Brings More Blessings to Men than Ignorance" and meaningfully employs two quotations from *Paradise Lost*, one being "Ye shall be as gods, knowing good and evil." We easily understand why the author praised ignorance! And the same magazine featured a 1790 piece, "An Oration, Intended to have been spoken, at a late Commencement, on the Unlawfulness and Impolicy of Capital Punishment, and the proper means of reforming criminals. By a Citizen of Maryland," which quotes from *Paradise Lost* and discusses its import to aid the author's thesis.

The way in which Milton is a presence in these early days of America may be seen in three issues of *The New Haven Gazette and the Connecticut Magazine* from 1788. One issue reprints and discusses "L'Allegro" and "Il Penseroso," being concerned with the presentation of nature in the poems. Another issue puts in a little story as filler, and recounts the frequently cited and amazing fact that Milton received only ten pounds total for

Paradise Lost. In a later issue we have a poem, "Vacation," which imitates the companion poems, not only in employing octosyllabic couplets and similar imagery, but in offering the first ten lines in parallel with Milton's first ten lines.

A significant component of presence always is literary allusion, but there is allusion that basically only name-drops and there is allusion that asks for intertextuality, asks for the reader to recall a rather full context of the former work to comprehend its communication for the current work. We must pause when in *The Life of Olaudah Equiano or Gustavus Vassa the African Written by Himself* (1789) we read: "Three shots were also fired at me and another boy, who was along with me, one of them in particular seemed—Wing'd with red lightning and impetuous rage—for, with a most dreadful sound it hissed close by me, and struck a rock at a little distance, which it shattered to pieces." Line 175 of book 1 of *Paradise Lost* is part of the Archfiend's first speech to Beelzebub rebutting his companion's weak acceptance of their fate in Hell. He notes that the vengeance of God that pursued them from Heaven has now drawn back, "and the Thunder,/ Wing'd with red Lightning and impetuous rage,/Perhaps hath spent his shafts, and ceases now." The French thus take on the posture of God or at least the assaulted English an analogue to the fallen devils, implying almost that Gustavus likens Satan and the other boy, Beelzebub. Not reading the allusion closely, we would conclude that the author wants us to side with the English, but that seems not to be so.

In the next chapter the author quotes *PL* 1.65–68, lines in which the narrator describes Hell, the place where "Hope never comes/That comes to all," Milton's variant on the legend of Dante's gate to Hell. The ship on which Gustavus is serving has reached the island of Montserrat in the West Indies, a "land of bondage," and he calls upon "God's thunder, and his avenging power, to direct the stroke of death," rather than let him again become a slave. The equation of slavery and Hell is underscored, but the narrative voice in the epic continues that "Such place Eternal Justice had prepar'd/For those rebellious." Gustavus does not lead the reader to believe he knows those words, but he must. For he persists without running away as others do, and so is rewarded by being sold to the benevolent Mr. Robert King, a Quaker, who soon takes Gustavus to his home in Philadelphia—and the etymological meaning of the city is demonstrated as the next stage in the account. An apostrophe to the Quakers and their helping of the oppressed African brethren appears in the last chapter.

The second to last sentence of the work is Adam's learning through the guidance of Michael; it is Gustavus's learning and his message to his reader: "After all, what makes any event important, unless by its observation we become better and wiser, and learn 'to do justly, to love mercy, and to walk humbly before God'?" (12.561–73.) These are only three of a number of allusions to Milton in the slave narrative, whose authorship has not been questioned. In any case, the presence of Milton in this particular early American narrative with its humanistic and basically abolitionist point of view says much about him as being emphatically American.

I would like to suggest another kind of presence for Milton, one that does not simply record allusions to him and quotations from him as do James Fennimore Cooper's novels, or employ direct ideas as Emerson does in his *Journals and Miscellaneous Notebooks* or in a poem like "Uriel," or imitate the poetry as specific poems by William Cullen Bryant or Edgar Allan Poe do. Rather I see the poet in the poem through the decisions the poet has made in forms or structures, language and imagery, the craft and the ideas or emotions that that craft sustains. The author is not dead when the poem takes on life, as some followers of Roland Barthes would like to believe: poetic presence is seen in the decisions creating the literary work, and that presence lives on unabated for readers who understand that such decisions have been made. If we understand this, then we are provided with a number of decisions which, in this case, the poet Milton made before writing or while writing, and these decisions point to his continuing presence as author.

For example, Milton divides the "Nativity Ode" into two parts, a four-stanza proem in rime royale and a 27-stanza hymn in eight lines of varied lengths. These elements then may be assigned to reasons of crafts, or symbolic meanings, and the choice of subject inclusions and exclusions directs the reader to the author's intentions. Here Milton does not deal with the flight to Egypt, does not focus on the birth descriptively; he does focus on the ultimate meaning of the birth in terms of the salvation that will come through Christ. And so in line 3 (with its numerological symbolism) we read, "Of wedded Maid, and Virgin Mother born"; we recognize a chiasmus, or X, for "wedded" goes with "Mother," and "Maid" goes with "Virgin," and we know that X is the sign of Christ (think of Xmas), the subject of the poem. Richard Crashaw made numerous other kinds of decisions in his nativity poem, and we can easily see that his presence is a very different kind of presence from Milton's. Therefore, we can point out that the presence of Milton as an American Milton may also lie in American authors' employment of Milton's influence in making their own decisions as they write, whereby Milton becomes a presence in their work.

That Miltonic presence may appear as it does in documents from the founding fathers, where no specific citation or allusion is given but where echo may occur, particularly when we know the author has been impressed by the thought or expression of the thought through some other means. One can be suspicious of interrelationships, as when in 1770 the first publication of a work by Milton appeared in the Colonies. This was *An Old Looking-Glass for the Laity and Clergy of all Denominations, Who either give or receive Money under Pretence of the Gospel: Being Considerations Touching The Likeliest Means to remove Hirelings out of the Church of Christ. Wherein are also discoursed of Tythes [etc.] by John Milton, Author of Paradise Lost. With a Life of Milton: Also large Extracts from his Works, concerning Bishops.* The occasion was the continued problem of tithing and liberty of conscience; and the excerpts are from *Animadversions Upon the Remonstrant's Defence, Of Reformation,* and *An Apology.* This came from the press of Robert Bell (who was to do the first poetic volumes in 1777), to be sold by J. Crukshank and I. Collins. *The Charter, Laws, and Catalogue of Books, of the Library Company of Philadelphia,* of which Ben Franklin was a founder, was published in 1764, with listings of Milton's complete prose, both epics, and Jonathan Richardson's *Explanatory Notes on Paradise Lost* with its important Life. Franklin and D. Hall were the printers. But in 1770 a new edition was printed by Joseph Crukshank, who also published successive editions; additions to the library are John Toland's *Life of Milton* and *History of Britain.* Further yet in 1770, in his *Public Advertiser* for 1 February, p. 4, Franklin reproduced a description of Chaos from Milton, and in *Father Abraham's Almanack, for the Year of Our Lord, 1770* there is "A Poem in Praise of the Married State," p. 21, drawn clearly from book 4 of *Paradise Lost.*

May we guess with fair reliance on just the preceding (and there are many more citations one can make for

Franklin and Milton) that Franklin as well as Jefferson and Adams knew Milton's work, both the major epic and some of the prose, and that his influence upon the thinking and documents of the new American government through these three alone also may reflect the presence of Milton? Is it not Milton, perhaps by way of Locke, who has written, "That to secure these rights, Governments are instituted among Men, deriving their just powers from the consent of the governed, That whenever any Form of Government becomes destructive of these ends, it is the Right of the People to alter or to abolish it, and to institute new Government"?

Milton's presence, as I have argued it, can be found in such naysayers as T. S. Eliot (much more than simply in the word *sylvan* in *The Waste Land)* and Hart Crane. It is of great importance for Ronald Johnson's work, even beyond his erased poem *RADI OS;* and for that major and magnificent and unfortunately little known epic, Louis Zukofsky's *A.*[2] Johnson's poem, incidentally, presents America as a paradise lost. Thus I would now like to glance at a few other authors who illustrate Milton's presence, as I have tried to define it, and through the ideas encased behind the writing itself, the presence makes clear why we can consider the American Milton in the terms Griswold implied.

Without the title, which is "Milton," and before we get to line 11, Henry Wadsworth Longfellow's Petrarchan sonnet, written in 1873, reveals Milton's presence to one familiar with his work. For this sonnet's long o's and a's so well reflect what Milton is doing in Sonnet 18, the so-called Piemont sonnet, "Avenge O Lord thy slaughter'd Saints":

> I pace the sounding sea-beach and behold
> > How the voluminous billows roll and run,
> > Upheaving and subsiding, while the sun

Shines through their sheeted emerald far unrolled,
And the ninth wave, slow gathering fold by fold
　All its loose-flowing garments into one,
　Plunges upon the shore, and floods the dun
　Pale reach of sands, and changes them to gold.
So in majestic cadence rise and fall
　The mighty undulations of thy song,
　O sightless bard, England's Maeonides!
And ever and anon, high over all
　Uplifted, a ninth wave superb and strong,
　Floods all the soul with its melodious seas.

Those organ sounds are not all that give us Milton's presence: note the enjambment, the interesting alliteration,
the accentuation of words in nonregular pattern. These
are not exclusive with Milton, of course, but they are
elements that sonneteers after him pick up and exploit,
and Longfellow specifically indicates that he is imitating
Milton's "mighty undulations."

One thus wonders whether Longfellow also was paying
attention to placement of reference, as Milton did in the
Piemont sonnet, for the number 11, that line when
England's Homer is cited, carries symbolism of regeneration and salvation, and the poem emphasizes the rolling
of the waves, reaching the ninth and strongest in the cycle,
a new cycle now beginning. (Milton's volta is in line nine;
the hundredth word is "hundred-fold" and alludes to the
parable of the sower; and eleven words follow that word
subtending concepts of salvation.) Milton in his works had
produced such a ninth wave, and now, Longfellow seems
to want us to understand, time has gone on to produce
another ninth wave that floods the soul of people today.
For Longfellow, it is a time of recognized achievement, the
production of *Christus* in 1872, and "Morituri Salutamus"
with the acknowledgment of the past and imminent death
but the uplifted flood of hope that those at the Bowdoin

College reunion, for which the poem was written, will continue achievement while the light remains.

Perhaps there is no direct Miltonic presence in Fredrick Goddard Tuckerman's sonnet of 1860 beginning "No! cover not the fault," but its alteration of the sonnet form in placement of the volta (or turn), its enjambment, its alliteration, and that elusive quality, its tone, all are *not* distanced from Milton's work. The thought is consistent with what we would think Milton would conceive. If Milton is not in fact a presence in the poem, his shade is:

> No! cover not the fault. The wise revere
> The judgement of the simple. harshly flow
> The words of counsel; but the end may show
> Matter and music to the unwilling ear.
> But perfect grief, like love, should cast out fear
> And like an o'erbrimmed river moaning go.
> Yet shrinks it from the senseless chaff and chat
> Of those who smile and insolently bestow
> Their ignorant praise, or those who stoop and peer
> To pick with sharpened fingers for a flaw,
> Nor ever touch the quick, nor rub the raw.
> Better than this were surgery rough as that
> Which, hammer and chisel in hand, at one sharp blow
> Strikes out the wild tooth from a horse's jaw.

Though he does not name Milton, Walt Whitman in *Democratic Vistas* avers

> that democracy can never prove itself beyond cavil, until it founds and luxuriantly grows its own forms of art, poems, schools, theology, displacing all that exists, or that has been produced anywhere in the past, under opposite in-fluences. . . . Our fundamental want to-day in the United States . . . is of a class, and the clear idea of a class, of native authors, literatures, far different, far higher in grade than any yet known, . . .

Well, there have been many arguments about what makes American literature American, but one influence, I feel sure, has been the American Milton. We find him in "The brave men, living and dead, who struggled here, have consecrated it, far above our poor power to add or detract," which reminds one of the thought of Sonnet 18, and in "It is for us the living, rather, to be dedicated to the great task remaining before us," a position Milton holds in all he wrote, particularly in the *First Defense* as he made clear in Sonnet 22. Margaret Fuller, as early as 1846, acknowledged the just and wise statement made by Griswold:

> Milton is American because in him is expressed so much of the primitive vitality of that thought from which America is born, though at present disposed to forswear her lineage in so many ways. . . . He understood the nature of liberty, of justice—what is required for the unimpeded action of conscience—what constitutes true marriage, and the scope of a manly education. He is one of the Fathers of the Age, . . . But the father is still far beyond the understanding of his child.

I suggest some children have understood, some like Adams and Lincoln and Fuller.

TEN

Milton's Joyce

The title of this chapter must strike the reader as backward, confused, strange. We usually think of, say, "Milton's Spenser" or "Joyce and Shakespeare," where the chronologically earlier author is seen as influence upon the later. Certainly a full study of Joyce's debts to Milton is due: it would summarize and expand the numerous articles that have been making us well aware of Joyce's relationship with Milton and his works,[1] the intertextuality that lies everywhere in Joyce's canon, and the anxieties of influence that we have come to appreciate, particularly in Joyce's psychological reaction which has, like T. S. Eliot's and Hart Crane's, tried to dismiss such "traditionism." And I trust such a full study is forthcoming.

But I would like to look at a different aspect of the relationship, one that exists for me as reader and student of both authors, one that thus in turn indicates the later author as critic and interpreter of the earlier. Succinctly, what I propose is to look at the way we can come to understand an earlier author—better? in different ways?—by understanding a later one who is dealing with the same

156

subjects and their expression. Part of that understanding—the righthand member of the equation—will, in the case of Joyce and Milton, be evidenced by allusion, by negative allusion, by commentary or quotation, by delving into literary structures or the same philosophic questions. But part of that understanding will also be the result of our being led into reconsiderations of the lefthand side of the equation by what we have otherwise come to know.

Not dissimilar, I suppose, is the view that quite rightly sees illustrators of Milton's poems, like William Blake or Carlotta Petrina, as readers and interpreters, giving us insights that had generally not been seen. And not dissimilar is Jorge Luis Borges's well-known perception from his remarks on Franz Kafka:

> The word "precursor" is indispensable in the vocabulary of criticism, but one should try to purify it from every connotation of polemic or rivalry. The fact is that each writer creates his precursors. His work modifies our conception of the past, as it will modify the future. In this correlation the identity or plurality of men matters not at all.[2]

Readers are aware of Joyce's employment of Milton's "Lycidas" in the Nestor section of *Ulysses*, his quotations and borrowed ideas. We understand Talbot's recitation of "Weep no more" as impinging on Stephen's remembrance of his mother's death and the resolution that Milton offers for death, loss, the incontrovertibles of life, the belief in the Christ and his ability to perform miracles, to bring salvation to the deserving. We recognize in Joyce's Milton that the "praise" will mount to heaven and counter the "blind *Fury's*" undeserved actions: Stephen can be assured, as he tells his students without quite yet understanding this point, that "the history" will come "After," that he too can hope for Fame, reward, though currently unaccomplished and unknown. But Stephen does not recognize this yet. He is at a point like that of the uncouth swain who ponders, "What boots it . . . To . . . strictly meditate the thankless muse." Stephen's resistence to Mr. Deasy's "All history moves towards one great goal, the manifestations of God," makes clear that he has not yet seen that "the history" will come "After," for it is still "a nightmare" and God but the reality of the shout in the street, "The harlot's cry" that William Blake and Oscar Wilde etched. Implied are "fresh woods and pastures new" once Stephen is able to turn "Full fathom five thy father lies" into "Sunk though he be beneath the watery floor." He will be so able as Proteus ends and we come to expect his path in the future to be one of accomplishment. While England and Victoria are an old hag with yellow teeth (Ezra Pound's "old bitch gone in the teeth"), there is that silent ship silently moving upstream, homing, with "sails brailed up on the crosstrees." The implication of the Christ and the crucifixion, with the metaphor of the body as a ship, now leaving the sea of life for an estuary leading to one's generational source, tells us that Milton's message is getting through. Joyce's Milton is thus enabling us to read Joyce's words more meaningfully, to read their implications, to understand what is happening to Stephen before it happens.

So armed, we discern the leavetaking of "Lycidas" earlier in "A cloud began to cover the sun slowly, shadowing the bay in deeper green," on p. 9 for Stephen and, later, more hidden, on p. 61 for Bloom: "A cloud began to cover the sun wholly slowly wholly" after the rain has been provoked and the Lord's Prayer, "On earth as it is in heaven," iterates Milton's/Joyce's statement of ultimate faith in history hereafter. As the reader of Yeats's poem "Who Goes With Fergus?" Stephen will, by novel's end, learn not to turn aside and brood on the bitter mysteries of life. Yeats asserts Fergus's power over "the shadows of the wood,/And the white breast of the dim sea/And all dishevelled wandering stars," and thus "no more" should the past and despair intrude. Joyce would have expected his reader, his fit audience, to recall these significant lines preceding those quoted in the novel—and so Stephen will learn to accept a position of "no more," turn from the past and stop brooding.

Yeats's line is repeated on p. 49 in the midst of discussion of Stephen's sexual self and his acceptance of himself as he is: "As I am. As I am. All or not at all." He, like Milton, will learn "Yet once more" and move forward. The reference in Milton, as in Yeats, is to Hebrews 12.25–29, where St. Paul admonishes that "much more shall not we escape, if we turn away from him that speaketh from heaven," and who says, "Yet once more I shake not the earth only, but also heaven. And this word, Yet once more, signifieth the removing of those things that are shaken, as of things that are made, that those which cannot be shaken may remain." For God is "a consuming fire." We have a rejection of those things of the past that are shaken, since they are of no consequence; we have an acceptance of those things that cannot be shaken as the only ones of consequence.

In Ithaca the first question is: "What parallel courses did Bloom and Stephen follow returning?" ("Returning" is important in this context.) We have Stephen's apparitions of his history, for example; we have the admiration for water and the phenomenon of ebullition through the agency of fire; we know Stephen's auditive sensation to be "in a profound ancient male unfamiliar melody the accumulation of the past" (do we sense "Lycidas" among others?), and Bloom's visual sensation to be "in a quick young male familiar form the predestination of a future" (the uncouth swain about to mature?). Evidenced is the irreparability of the past (which thus demands its acknowledgment and acceptance and finally sublimation); in "the birth or death of other persons" are perceived "the attendant phenomena of eclipses, solar and lunar, from immersion to emersion, . . . persistence of infernal light, obscurity of terrestrial waters, pallor of human beings"; and it is Stephen, victim of Bloom's "postcenal gymnastic display," who is the salient point of the narration. In the apparitions of history are the uncouth swain's and Stephen's dwelling on the things that are shakeable and shaken. The water imagery of the "Galilean lake" and the tenth verse paragraph of "Lycidas" echo in Proteus and the contrastive lake of the Proteus episode. In the "sudden blaze," "the swart star," "the day star" that "with newspangled ore/Flames in the forehead of the morning sky" of "Lycidas" is the ebullition of the fire (the consuming fire that is God) that will produce "fresh woods and pastures new." The uncouth swain learns to pass beyond the mere approval of Damoetas old to a Doric lay; he learns that the "fatall and perfidious bark" (the ship as body metaphor) was "Built in th' eclipse," and that the "two-handed engine" "Stands ready to smite once and smite no more."

Milton's lines are like a Joycean answer to the question "Which various features of the constellations were in turn considered?" (The last two words of Milton's line "Stands ready to smite once and smite no more," incidentally, recall the first three of the poem as well as the first two words of book 9 of *Paradise Lost*, in which the Fall is recounted. What Yeats's reader and Stephen need to encompass is the reality of the Fall, and Stephen's sexual preoccupations reflect what is its reality from a male point of view.) There is a play of light intensity in the persistence of infernal light mobilizing *Paradise Lost* and *Finnegans Wake*, against the pallor of human beings that follows Bloom's "A cloud began to cover the sun wholly slowly wholly": "Grey," "No wind would lift those waves, grey metal, poisonous foggy waters," "A dead sea in a dead land, grey and old," "the grey sunken cunt of the world," "Grey horror [that] seared his flesh"—and we recall earlier Buck Mulligan's citation of Algy (with context and color puns) Swinburne's "grey sweet mother, the snotgreen sea." And there is a play of light intensity against the "obscurity" of terrestial things felt by the unheralded swain and unrecognized Stephen. The message to the reader—that is, to Stephen; that is, to Joyce—that is sustained by Bloom's catechism relating his position in bed with Molly is contained in the answer to "If he had smiled why would he have smiled?":

> To reflect that each one who enters imagines himself to be the first to enter whereas he is always the last term of a preceding series even if the first term of a succeeding one, each imagining himself to be first, last, only and alone, whereas he is neither first nor last nor only nor alone in a series originating in and repeated to infinity.

That, read alongside "Lycidas," tells us much about that poem and even more about the Milton who was to write *Paradise Lost* for fit audience though few and *Paradise Regain'd* for the chosen children of Adam, those of humankind to be saved by inculcating the heroic action of the Son.

Although Milton and his work do not emerge specifically in the Ithaca chapter, there is an intertextual presence; yet it is more observable in the way in which some of the concepts and imagery of that catechism inform Milton's poems rather than the other way around. It is as if we can better understand one of the high points in that series of smiles (that is, *Paradise Lost*) as humankind overviews life by understanding another and later high point in that series of smiles (that is, *Ulysses*). We understand that the obscure swain who touched the tender stops of various quills while the still morn went out with sandals gray has learned that the Sun that has dropt into the western bay will indeed repair his dropping head and trick his beams and flame in the forehead of the morning sky. The circularity of Poldy and Molly and the efflorescence of name and identification of Earth Mother underscore that.

The agreement of Milton with Joyce that indeed human life is infinitely perfectible and that there are generic conditions imposed by natural law, integral to the human whole, even involving pain and cataclysms and supposedly distasteful human conditions, was a conclusion I reached some time ago in examining the graphic symbolism of *Paradise Lost*:

> The myth of exodus is plainly an archetype of birth; its stages through history are the movement of generations through history, each, it is hoped, an advance over the preceding generation. . . . A modern example of this use of exodus can be seen in Joyce's *A Portrait of the Artist as a Young Man*, a novel which is a womb in which the gestation of its hero is expressed in imagery following the course of pregnancy. The novel ends with the exodus of Stephen Dedalus from his maternal life—from mother and country—to a world to be forged into the artifacts of immortality.[3]

That had not been a way in which *Paradise Lost* had been read: it is not a tragedy, though it engage the tragic mode at times as in book 9. Had critics paid attention to the catechistic question of Ithaca, "What would render such return irrational?", they might have perceived a reading of the epic different from tradition's. The answer to the question is: "An unsatisfactory equation between an exodus and return in space through irreversible time." But of course such return is *not* irrational, because exodus and return in irreversible time and in reversed space *can* achieve a satisfactory equation (as "Exiles" on a personal level and *Finnegans Wake* on a mythic level demonstrate).

The "message" of "Lycidas" involves this same rational equation between the exodus from his former life that the uncouth swain is contemplating and the return to the literary world of achievement toward which time will lead him. Much depends, though, on that word "unsatisfactory." When we understand "Lycidas," Yeats's Fergus, or Joyce's Stephen, we know that the equation will depend upon the hopes and the achievements. The darkened circle ending the Ithaca chapter and answering the question "Where?" provides restatement of the satisfactory answer. The circle is a black dot, a darkened circle, a seeming ending, but also the punctuation completing Molly's "Yes." It is, I suggest, a pictorialization of the eclipse of the sun, which has been evoked before, with its Christological world to come as a result of the redemption: as a result, that is, of the Penelope chapter. The answer to the question is both the circularity of Poldy and Molly's positions in their square bed, and the squared circle of the preceding answer, with its allusion to the circularity associated with God and to the square of Heaven (Revelation 21.15–17), the miraculousness of a squared circle, and most importantly the eclipse of the sun. Here in the darkened circle we have "Darkinbad" and "the Brightdayler." It serves, indeed, as a gloss upon Milton's lines in "Comus":

> He that has light within his own cleer brest
> May sit i'th center, and enjoy bright day,
> But he that hides a dark soul, and foul thoughts
> Benighted walks under the noonday sun;
> Himself is his own dungeon.

One does not hide the dark soul; one broods upon the dark Abyss and mak'st it pregnant with Dove-like creatures. What is in one dark is illumined.

Notes

NOTES TO INTRODUCTION

1. *A Variorum Commentary on the Poems of John Milton*, ed. A.S.P., Woodhouse and Douglas Bush (New York: Columbia University Press, 1972), 2.1.174.

NOTES TO CHAPTER ONE

1. Alwin Thaler, "The Shaksperean Element in Milton," *Shakspere's Silences* (Cambridge: Harvard University Press, 1929), 154, n. 1. See also *PMLA* 40 (1925): 645–91; "Shakespeare and Milton Once More," *SAMLA Studies in Milton*, ed. J. Max Patrick (Gainesville: University of Florida Press, 1953), 80–99; and "Shakespearean Recollection in Milton: A Summing Up," *Shakespeare and Our World* (Knoxville: University of Tennessee Press, 1966), 139–227.

2. Henry John Todd, ed., *The Poetical Works of John Milton* (London, 1801), six volumes. Reference will be found in the editions cited at the Miltonic or Shakespearean locus.

3. Thomas Newton, ed., *Paradise Regain'd, To Which is Added Samson Agonistes and Poems Upon Several Occasions* (London, 1752).

4. See Ethel Seaton, "*Comus* and Shakespeare," *Essays and Studies* 31 (1945): 68–80.

5. See Hanmer's edition of *The Works of William Shakespeare; Carefully Reviewed and Corrected from the Former Editions* (London, 1743–44).

6. Charles Dunster, ed., *Paradise Regained, a Poem. with Notes of Various Authors* (London, 1800).

7. Thomas P. Harrison, "The 'Broom–Groves' in *The Tempest,"* *Shakespeare Association Bulletin* 20 (1945): 39–45.

8. David Masson, ed., *The Poetical Works of John Milton* (London, 1874), three volumes; see vol. 3 for notes.

9. George Coffin Taylor, *Milton's Use of Du Bartas* (Cambridge: Harvard University Press, 1934).

10. Sanford Golding, "The Sources of the *Theatrum Poetarum,"* *PMLA* 76 (1961): 48–53.

11. References are: David Masson, *The Life of John Milton* (London, 1859–74), vol. 1; Ernest Brennecke, *John Milton the Elder and His Music* (New York: Columbia University Press, 1938); Francis Peck, *New Memoirs of the Life and Writings of John Milton* (London, 1742); Newton, "Life of John Milton," *Paradise Lost* (London, 1749).

12. Robert Metcalf Smith, *The Variant Issues of Shakespeare's Second Folio and Milton's First Published Poem: a Bibliographical Problem* (Bethlehem, Pa.: Lehigh University, 1928).

13. Morris Freedman, "Milton's 'On Shakespeare' and Henry Lawes," *Shakespeare Quarterly* 14 (1963): 279–81.

14. Theodore Spencer, "Shakespeare and Milton," *Modern Language Notes* 53 (1938): 366–67.

15. John Guillory, *Poetic Authority: Spenser, Milton, and Literary History* (New York: Columbia University Press, 1983), 19.

16. A. W. Verity, ed., *Milton's "Ode on the Morning of Christ's Nativity," "L'Allegro," "Il Penseroso," and "Lycidas"* (Cambridge, 1891). For Malone, see *The Plays and Poems of William Shakespeare* (London, 1790; revised, 1821); for Bowles, see Thomas Warton's second edition of *Poems Upon Several Occasions* (London, 1791).

17. Margaret B. Pickel, *Charles I as Patron of Poetry and Drama* (London, 1936).

18. See the following: Warton, ed., *Poems on Several Occasions* (London, 1785); Skeat, trans., *John Milton. Lament for Damon and Other Latin poems* (Oxford: Oxford University Press, 1935); Langdon, *Milton's Theory of Poetry and Fine Art* (New Haven: Yale University Press, 1924); Hurd, Newton's variorum edition (1752); Keightley, ed., *The Poems of John Milton* (London, 1859), two volumes; and Sampson, ed., *The Lyric and Dramatic Poems of John Milton* (London: Bell, 1901).

19. See the following: Furnivall, *Some 300 Fresh Allusions to Shakspere* (London, 1885); Munro, *Shakespeare Allusion*

book (London, 1909), vol. 1; St. John, ed., *The Prose Works of John Milton* (London, 1872).

20. For George Steevens, see Malone's variorum; for Hales, see "Milton's Macbeth," *Beiblatt* 2 (1892): 278 [also, *Eclectic Magazine* 118 (1892): 230–32; *Nineteenth Century* 30 (1891): 919–32; *Living Age* 77 (1892): 431–39; *Folia Litteraria* (New York, 1893), 198–219].

21. See Elsie Duncan-Jones, "Milton's Late Court Poet," *Notes & Queries* N.S. 1 (1954): 473.

22. Paul Stevens, *Imagination and the Presence of Shakespeare in Paradise Lost* (Madison: University of Wisconsin Press, 1985).

23. Grant McColley, *Paradise Lost: An Account of Its Growth and Major Origins, with a Discussion of Milton's Use of Sources and Literary Patterns* (Chicago: Packard and Co., 1940).

24. Commentators noted here but not previously cited in this essay are: O. G. Gilchrist, [annotations], *Monthly Magazine* 13 (1802): 346–49; G. Wilson Knight, *Chariot of Wrath: The Message of John Milton to Democracy at War* (London: Faber and Faber, 1942); V. R., "Milton's Asclepiadean Verses," *Notes & Queries* 163 (1932): 371; Henry H. Adams, "The Development of the Flower Passage in *Lycidas*," *Modern Language Notes* 65 (1950): 468–72; Peter Whalley, *An Enquiry into the Learning of Shakespeare with Remarks on Several Passages of His Plays* (London, 1748); E. B. Seymour, *Remarks, Critical, Conjectural, and Explanatory, Upon the Plays of Shakespeare* (London, 1805), two vols.; Merritt Y. Hughes, ed., *The Complete Poetry and Major Prose of John Milton* (Indianapolis: Odyssey Press, 1957); William Sidney Walker, *A Critical Examination of the Text of Shakespeare* (London, 1860), three vols.; Percy Allen, *Shakespeare, Jonson, and Wilkins as Borrowers* (London, 1928); John Callander, ed., Milton's *Paradise Lost, Book 1* (Glasgow, 1750); anonymous: see Shakspere Society of Philadelphia, *Notes of Studies on the Tempest* (Philadelphia, 1866); Douglas Bush, *Mythology and the Renaissance Tradition in English Poetry* (Minneapolis: University of Minnesota Press, 1932).

25. The words are Thaler's.

26. The aside may be one of the best indications that the Castlehaven scandal does have relevancy to the masque. See Barbara Breasted, "*Comus* and the Castlehaven Scandal," *Milton Studies* 3 (1971): 201–04, and compare John Creasor, "Milton's *Comus:* The Irrelevance of the Castlehaven Scandal," *Notes &*

Queries N.S. 31 (1984): 307–17.

27. John Cleland, *Memoires of a Woman of Pleasure* (London, 1749), vol. 2 (The Second Letter): 61.

28. See the important study by John Hollander, *The Figure of Echo: A Mode of Allusion in Milton and After* (Berkeley: University of California Press, 1981).

29. See *With Mortal Voice: The Creation of Paradise Lost* (Lexington: University Press of Kentucky, 1984), 68–70.

30. Richard J. Du Rocher, *Milton and Ovid* (Ithaca: Cornell University Press, 1985), 36.

31. See also Mephostophilis's "Why this is hell, nor am I out of it" (Marlowe, *Dr. Faustus* 1.3.75) and numerous other lines. Satan's relationship to Marlowe's play and others is discussed by Helen Gardner in *A Reading of Paradise Lost* (Oxford: Clarendon Press, 1965), "Appendix A: Milton's Satan and the Theme of Damnation in Elizabethan Tragedy," 99–120.

32. *Julius Caesar* 3.1.270–73/*PL* 10.616–17; cited by Newton, although Thaler credits Verity. If there is a Shakespearean remembrance here, it joins *FQ* 6.8.49 and 6.11.16–17. The Dogs of Hell will also be found in Apollonius Rhodius IV, 1666.

Notes to Chapter Two

1. Edward Dowden, "Milton in the Eighteenth Century (1701–1750)." Separate reprint from the *Proceedings of the British Academy* 3 (1908): 275–94; delivered 10 December 1908.

2. John W. Good, *Studies in the Milton Tradition* (Urbana: University of Illinois Press, 1915; reprinted, New York: Johnson Reprint Co., 1967).

3. George W. Sherburn, "The Early Popularity of Milton's Minor Poems," *Modern Philology* 17 (1919–20): 259–78, 515–40.

4. Raymond Dexter Havens, *The Influence of Milton on English Poetry* (Cambridge: Harvard University Press, 1922; reprinted, New York: Russell & Russell, 1961).

5. John T. Shawcross, *Milton: The Critical Heritage* (London: Routledge & Kegan Paul, 1970), 23, 25.

6. John T. Shawcross, *Milton 1732–1801: The Critical Heritage* (London: Routledge & Kegan Paul, 1972), 19.

7. Marjorie Hope Nicolson, *John Milton: A Reader's Guide to His Poetry* (New York: Noonday Press, 1963), 257.

8. Nancy Lee-Riffe, "Milton in the Eighteenth-Century

Periodicals: Hail, Wedded Love!" *Notes & Queries* N.S. 12 (1965): 18–19.

9. Morris Golden, "A Decade's Bent: Names in the *Monthly Review* and the *Critical Review*, 1760–1769," *Bulletin of the New York Public Library* 79 (1976): 336–61.

NOTES TO CHAPTER THREE

1. James Thorpe, *Milton Criticism: Selections from Four Centuries* (New York: Rinehart, 1950), 5, 6.

2. Thorpe, 6.

3. Peter Hägin, *The Epic Hero and the Decline of Heroic Poetry: A Study of the Neoclassical English Epic with special reference to Milton's Paradise Lost* (Bern: Francke, 1964), Chapter 5: "The Hero of Paradise Lost," 146–49.

4. Dustin Griffin, *Regaining Paradise: Milton and the Eighteenth Century* (Cambridge: Cambridge University Press, 1986).

5. See remarks in Lecture 14, pp. 99–100; Lecture 20, pp. 151–52, 161; Lecture 21, p. 174; Lecture 22, p. 185; Lecture 27, pp. 235–36; Lecture 28, p. 246; Lecture 29, p. 248; Lecture 32, pp. 283–84; Lecture 33, pp. 290–91; Lecture 34, pp. 303, 304–05.

6. See W. Hooper's translation, section 2, chapters 12 and 20; and section 8, chapters 14 and 19.

7. See pp. 29, 34, 52, 86, 88, 100, 107–08, 122, 125, 146–47, 167. Lowth frequently discusses Richard Bentley's "corrections" of the text of *Paradise Lost* (1732).

8. References and quotations are drawn from *Eikonoklastes, Paradise Lost*, and "Comus"; see volume 1; book 2, chapter 6; book 3, chapter 1; volume 2; book 1; chapters 1 and 7; volume 3: book 1, chapters 1, 3, 5, and 8; and the Conclusion.

9. See the edition published in Northampton, Massachusetts, by Thomas M. Pomroy (1804), 57–58 and note.

10. Printed in *Selectorum Litterariorum Pentas Continens Dissertationes Historico-morales* (Leipzig, 1730), 28, 70–71. Neither author is mentioned by Leo Miller in *John Milton Among the Polygamophiles* (New York: Loewenthal Press, 1974).

11. See pp. 48, 183.

12. See *Of the Origin and Progress of Language* (Edinburgh, 1774), 2:357.

13. "On the Utility of Classical Learning," 1:739.

14. *Lectures on Rhetoric and Belles Lettres* (London, 1759), Lecture 4.

15. "Dialogues of the Dead," No. 14 (between Pope and Boileau).

NOTES TO CHAPTER FOUR

1. Wordsworth's remarks, of course, are found in his preface to the *Lyrical Ballads* (1800).

2. Compare Gerald Wester Chapman's statement in *Literary Criticism in England, 1660–1800* (New York: Alfred Knopf, 1966), 5–6: "The story of eighteenth-century criticism requires a converging double plot, in which eroding orthodoxy passes almost imperceptibly into constrained revolution; in which ancient code, which has always to be rediscovered and restated, acts as a civilizing, complicating brake upon new codes, which have painfully to be invented."

3. Among the most important influences in effecting this change was Peter Ramus, whose work in logic has been thoroughly analyzed by Walter Ong, S. J., in *Ramus, Method and the Decay of Dialogue* (Cambridge: Harvard University Press, 1958); *Rhetoric, Romance, and Technology* (Ithaca: Cornell University Press, 1971); *Complete Prose Works of John Milton* (New Haven: Yale University Press, 1982), 8:141–205. Various scholars have studied the significance of Ramist logic for Milton; see Father Ong's essay "Logic & the Epic Muse: Reflections on Noetic Structures in Milton's Milieu" in *Achievements of the Left Hand: Essays in Milton's Prose* (Amherst: University of Massachusetts Press, 1974), ed. Michael Lieb and John T. Shawcross, 265–66, n. 1. The essay summarizes much of the scholarship and comments significantly on its importance for *Paradise Lost*.

4. *The Scholemaster* (1570): "This *Imitatio* is *dissimilis materiei similis tractatio*; and, also, *similis materiei dissimilis tractatio*."

5. With the remarks of Thomas Hobbes in his preface to Sir William Davenant's *Gondibert* (1651), we have a clear statement of one aspect of what this philosophic change to systematization meant for literature. It became an epitome of what was to dominate the next century and a half, and it offered a kind of scaffolding upon which authors could imitate older (classical) writers

169

who produced poems with certain generic names and certain intentionalities. And when the eighteenth century was just about to begin, the then and now little read William Wollaston, typical of the age and the lesser writer, talked of such matters in the preface to his dull poem on Ecclesiastes: "The principal kinds of Poems are, either those that tend to *the advancement of Vertue*: as, *the Epic Poem*, which set before us the achievements of those, that have been famous and Heroic, as patterns for others in their circumstances: *Tragedy*, which teaches us not to over-value or rely upon temporal advantages, by the falls of those who have had the most of them; to be tender-hearted, by using to pity their misfortunes; to be couragious, by evoking at their patience; and to be humble, by observing what the greatest of men may come to: *Ode*, that excites our devotion, by singing the attributes of the Deity; or a laudable emulation, by celebrating the praises of some Worthy: *Eclogue*, that continues a pious remembrance of the deceased Friends of our Country, of Learning, or our selves: Or those, on the contrary, that tend *to depress and discredit Vice*: as *Comedy*, which presents to view the faults of common Conversations: and *Satyr*, which by its arguments exposes, not so much men, as their unreasonableness and enormities" (*The Design of Part of the Book of Ecclesiastes* [London, 1691], 7–8). Not only do we find the limiting concepts of narrow genres, but the statement manifests the importance of the didactic mode. And although his poem was influenced by *Paradise Lost*, as he acknowledges in his preface, it is written in rhyming couplets, as were Samuel Wesley's *The Life of Our Blessed Lord and Savior Jesus Christ* (1693), and Sir Richard Blackmore's *Prince Arthur* (1695) and *King Arthur* (1697), also products of Milton's influence through the epic. Marvell's heroic couplets praising Milton's poem are prosodically typical, but as he presents them, they praise more by eschewing competition with Milton's blank verse. Wentworth Dillon, the Earl of Roscommon's blank verse encomium inserted into his rhymed "An Essay on Translated Verse" (1685) is all the more amazing when one considers the question of prosody.

6. From "Life of Milton," *Prefaces, Biographical and Critical to the Works of the English Poets* (1779), vol. 60 of *Works* and vol. 2 of *Prefaces*; quoted from John T. Shawcross, ed., *Milton 1732–1801: The Critical Heritage* (London: Routledge & Kegan Pual, 1972), 293–94, 297, hereafter cited as *Milton*, vol. 2.

7. This attitude is basically what underlies Addison's and

Voltaire's criticism of the Sin and Death allegory of book 2 in *Paradise Lost*: it simply was not appropriate or decorous for the poem that *they* read. Ultimately, of course, what the objectors to this passage are saying is that Sin and Death are abstractions and the other characters of the poem—Satan, and Adam and Eve, and God the Father and the Son, and the angels—are not. But that is just the point: all are abstractions and the almost universal reading of *Paradise Lost*, that rendered by a God-believing and Bible-believing public, has been quite wrong. The misreading of what Milton, certainly a God-believer and Bible-believer, created as copyist has led to the meaningless arguments over Satan and the figure of God: readers of the poem have looked at what they thought was Milton's "imitating" in an Aristotelian sense when what he presented was what he "copied" in a Platonic sense. (See later for this distinction between Aristotelian and Platonic approaches to a poetic.)

The point can be made with other examples. Twentieth century critics have misread Henry Vaughan frequently through a reversed confusion: we hear so often that Vaughan wrote great first lines but that then the poem falls apart. Such critics reflecting a "romantic" view–and Vaughan has been tied to Wordsworth fairly often and without foundation—condemn Vaughan for not presenting the vision they think the poem was written to present, and thereby do not pay attention to Vaughan's structures, total concept, employment of imitative materials. Vaughan is simply not the emotionalist working out the poem as it proceeds as some have tried to see him: he is a "maker" in the way that Jonson, one of his two most important influences, used the term. (The other important influence was George Herbert.)

8. Quoted from John T. Shawcross, ed., *Milton: The Critical Heritage* (London: Routledge & Kegan Paul, 1970), 257, hereafter cited as Milton, vol. 1.

9. *Milton*, vol. 2, p. 66.

10. *Milton*, vol. 1, p. 264.

11. *Milton and the Line of Vision*, ed. Joseph A. Wittreich (Madison: University of Wisconsin Press, 1975).

12. Compare Thomas McFarland's discussion of what he calls "The Originality Paradox" in *New Literary History* 5 (1973–1974): 447–76. "The recognition of the originality paradox by classical antiquity, as well as our recognition of its presence in forms of culture other than the merely poetic, comes together on a common ground, and is unified in its meaning, in

the historical nexus of Plato's rejection of the 'imitative poets' as inhabitants of his ideal society" (465). By "originality paradox" McFarland means the sharp polarity between the individual author and the tradition that has become the pedagogics of his age, even though it is from such a society that the author draws his substance.

13. In *The Poetry of Vision: Five Eighteenth-Century Poets* [Thomson, Collins, Gray, Smart, Cowper] (Cambridge: Harvard University Press, 1967), Patricia Meyer Spacks discusses poetic "air-formed visions" in distinction from the more frequent imitative quality of eighteenth century poetry; such "vision" arises "between the world of the poet and that of normal human experience," through the alteration of actuality in order to try to render it.

14. Compare the comment of Ricardo Quintana and Alvin Whitley in *English Poetry of the Mid and Late Eighteenth Century* (New York: Alfred Knopf, 1963): "The individual was seen as responding to the messages conveyed to him by his senses from the outside world; the artist embodied this sense data in the imagery of the work of art; the reader of the poem or the viewer of the painting or sculpture experienced the work sensationalistically as he would any other object outside himself" (7–8).

15. The words are Richard Poirier's, talking of Byron, Yeats, and Lawrence in *The Performing Self* (New York: Oxford University Press, 1971), 86.

16. Paul S. Sherwin, in *Precious Bane: Collins and the Milton Legacy* (Austin: University of Texas Press, 1977), calls it an "antistrophe" (26), and the second section, a "mesode" (19). Section 3 is similar in form to and contrastive in substance with section 1 (the strophe), and section 2 might better be considered the epode, as in Collins's "Ode to Liberty," which has four sections labeled strophe, epode, antistrophe, and second epode.

17. Hägin, *The Epic Hero.*

18. While the poem does suggest such dichotomizing, echoes from Milton—Sherwin points them out—in the "Beauty" sections indicate that it is not a simple either/or poetical character that is being delineated, and *The Faerie Queene* can hardly be barred from the sublime. Spenser is often "inwardturning" and gives us "poetry of prophetic vision"; and once one acknowledges the allegoric substruct of the entire epic, *Paradise Lost* takes on "outwardgoing" properties.

19. I quote from the fourth edition, an autographed copy of

which is owned by the University of Kentucky Library, although the National Union Catalogue lists no copy in this country.

NOTES TO CHAPTER FIVE

1. Dustin Griffin, *Regaining Paradise: Milton and the Eighteenth Century* (Cambridge: Cambridge University Press, 1986), 2.
2. Joseph Wittreich, *Feminist Milton* (Ithaca: Cornell University Press, 1987).
3. William Godwin, *An Enquiry concerning Political Justice* (Dublin, 1793), 1:241. "[Satan] bore his torments with fortitude, because he disdained to be subdued by despotic power. He sought revenge, because he could not think with tameness of the unexpostulating authority that assumed to dispose of him. How beneficial and illustrious might the temper from which these qualities flowed have proved with a small diversity of situation!" Godwin's further words (242) suggest Caleb Williams was already in his mind: "A man of quick resentment, of strong feelings, and who pertinaciously resists every thing that he regards as an unjust assumption, may be considered as having in him the seeds of eminence."

NOTES TO CHAPTER SIX

1. There are significant references to Milton's works in the novel. See the letter to George Mordaunt from H. Mandeville, 1:51: "like the fallen angel in Milton, I felt [quotation of *PL* 4.847–48]"; the letter to Colonel Bellville from Wilmot, 1:57: "*Il divono Enrico* is a little in the *penseroso*"; the letter to Mordaunt from H. Mandeville, 1:60: "I kissed . . . which called up into her cheeks a blush 'Celestial rosie red' [*PL* 8.619], implying "Loves proper hue"; the letter to Bellville from Wilmot, 2.212: "the loveliest pair" (*PL* 4.321); and the letter to Colonel Bellville from Lady Anne Wilmot, 2:219, where the last two sentences are drawn from *PL* 7.610 ("easily the proud attempt/Of Spirits apostat and thir Counsels vain/Thou hast repeld").
2. For Miltonic allusions see chapter 2, p. 11 ("L'Allegro," 134); chapter 4, p. 25 (reference to *Paradise Lost*); chapter 17, p. 103 (*PL* 3.348); chapter 18 p. 107 (reference, citation, and adaptation

of *PL* 8.591–92); and chapter 19, p. 118 (use of *PL* 1.63).

3. Ann Messenger, *His and Hers: Essays in Restoration and Eighteenth Century Literature* (Lexington: University Press of Kentucky, 1986).

Notes to Chapter Seven

1. Edmund Burke, *A Letter to John Farr and John Harris Esqrs., Sheriffs of the City of Bristol, on the Affairs of America* (1777) in B. W. Hill, ed., *Edmund Burke On Government, Politics and Society* (New York: International Publications Service, 1976), p. 198.

2. Richard Price, *Discourse on the Love of Our Country* (1790), cited in Burke's *Reflections on the Revolution in France, and on the Proceedings in Certain Societies in London relative to that Event: in a Letter intended to have been sent to a Gentleman in Paris* (1790), quoted from Hill, p. 280.

3. Hill, 320, 330, 350.

4. Hill, 353.

5. Hill, 294.

6. Keith Michael Baker, ed., *Condorcet: Selected Writings* (Indianapolis: Bobbs-Merrill, 1976), 223, and 222.

7. Baker, 145, 146, 182.

8. *Tenure of Kings and Magistrates*, 26, and *Eikonoklastes*, 46.

9. *Pro populo Anglicano defensio*, p. 2; Yale Prose, 4:326–27, translated by Donald MacKenzie.

10. See also Keith W. F. Stavely's introduction to his edition of *Of True Religion* in the Yale Prose, vol. 8 and a forthcoming essay on that tract, in which I detail Locke's debt to it in *Two Treatises*.

11. Quoted from *French and English Philosophers* (New York: P. F. Collier & Son, 1938), volume 34 of The Harvard Classics: 216–17.

12. Letter 1 in Antoine Louis Claude Destutt de Tracy, translated by Thomas Jefferson, *A Commentary and Review of Montesquieu's Spirit of Laws* (1811), reprinted New York: Burt Franklin (1969), 285.

13. See *Milton 1732–1801: The Critical Heritage* (London: Routledge & Kegan Paul, 1972), 30–31, 38. The reference to Batteux is to *Principes de la littérature. Nouvelle édition* (Paris, 1764), 2:206–08, first published in 1756.

14. Jean Gillet, *Le Paradis perdu dans la littérature française De Voltaire à Chateaubriand* (Paris: Libraire Klincksieck, 1975), chapter 11, pp. 483–556; see 483–484. "Personne ne montre plus la moindre sympathie pour l'activité politique de Milton. L'attitude de Mosneron est a cet égard exemplaire: en 1788, celui-ci faisant un éloge discret du civisme du poète et de son goût pour la liberté. En 1804, il blâme sévèrement le factieux Milton."

15. *Lycée* 13 and 14 (Paris, 1804); see Gillet, 493. "Satan announce son intention de surpasser les crimes des Anglais 'parricides' et de Cromwell, et lorsqu'il apparaît à Danton en songe, c'est sous la figure du Protecteur."

NOTES TO CHAPTER EIGHT

1. See Voltaire, *An Essay Upon the Civil Wars of France, Extracted from Curious Manuscripts. And also Upon the Epick Poetry of the European Nations from Homer Down to Milton* (London, 1727), especially 102–30, with comment on *L'Adamo* on 103; and *An Essay . . . The Second Edition, Corrected by Himself* (London, 1728), same paging.

2. See the manuscript letter in the extra-illustrated copy of Samuel Weller Singer's edition of Spence's *Anecdotes, Observations, and Characters, of Books and Men* (London, 1820), in the Henry E. Huntington Library, RB 131213.

3. Hayley refers to Walker's *Historical Memoirs of the Irish Bards* (Dublin, 1786).

4. See Goldsmith's *An Enquiry into the Present State of Polite Learning in Europe* (London, 1759), 48.

5. See *The Monthly Review* 14 (1794): 235, and *The Critical Review* 16 (1796): 488–90.

6. See *The British Critic* 3 (1794): 172–77.

7. See *Prose, e Poesie Del Signor Abate Antonio Conti Patrizio Veneto* (Venezia, 1739–1756), two volumes; 2 (1756): xciii-xcv, 78, 133, 229.

8. *Discorsi Accademici di Anton Maria Salvini Detti da Lui nell'Accademia degli Apatisti. Con Alcune due Traduzioni dal Greco. Parte Terza* (Firenze, 1733), "Discorso XXI," 63.

9. See Letter 67, II, 181–83, in *Delle Lettere Familiari del Conti Lorenzo Magalotti* (Firenze, 1769), two volumes.

10. See *Fasti Consolari dell'Accademia Fiorentina* (Firenze, 1717), "Consolo CXX," 554.

11. See *Opera Varie* (Venice, 1757), two volume; 2:367–68, 427, 408, respectively as well as p. 96 ("Dialogo Quarto: Nel Quale si continua ad esporre il sistema di Ottica del neutono"). Later editions are *Opere del Conti Algarotti* (Cremona, 1778–1779), five volumes, and *Opere* (Venezia, 1791–1794), ten volumes.

12. See *Scelta delle Piu'Bella Ed Utili Speculazioni Inglesi dello Spettatore, Ciarlatore, e Tutore Tradotti in Italiano* (Livorno, 1753), "Ciarlatore," no. 263, pp. 340–41.

13. William Riley Parker suggests that the other edition was published in Italy in 1759—*Milton: A Biography* (Oxford: Clarendon Press, 1968), 2:829. See Samuel Kliger, "Milton in Italy and the Lost Malatesti Manuscript," *Studies in Philology* 51 (1954): 208–13, for an important discussion of the manuscripts and printings of *La Tina*.

14. Kliger cites two editions with differing title pages, one dated, one undated, and indicates that both were probably published in London as stated. The original manuscript of a copy was given to Giovanni Marsili, a visitor to England from the University of Padua. Neither this copy nor that sent to the Della Crusca Academy has been discovered, although a letter from Hollis, dated 2 June 1761, in Italian and in English translation, indicates the gift of the manuscript and a five-volume edition of Milton's works and John Toland's *Life*. Francis Blackburne in his life of Hollis dated this 26 September 1758. The Biblioteca Riccardiana has two letters from Marsili to Lami, dated 6 June and 4 September 1758, concerning the manuscript. There is another holograph manuscript of the sonnets, however, in the Biblioteca Nazionale Centrale in Florence (Class VIII, Codex 253) in the Magliabachi Collection, dedicated to Francesco Cordoni; it is dated 1650. (After Hollis's death, Brand, his primary heir, legally took the name Hollis; there has been some confusion, therefore, in accounts of this episode.)

15. *Thraliana. The Diary of Mrs. Hester Lynch Thrale (Later Mrs. Piozzi) 1776–1809*, ed. Katherine C. Balderston (Oxford: Clarendon Press, 1942); see entries dated from February 1780 to 16 August 1786, 1:425–26, 443, 465, 536, 591, 611, 663. Entries before and after those dates also include discussions or citations of Milton. She and her husband went to Italy shortly after their

marriage, soon going to Florence where she became friends with Merry and joined the "Della Cruscans," as they were called.

16. It might also be pointed out that Robert, Viscount Hampden and Baron Trevor, wrote a poem in Latin called "Britannia," dated 1761, with six lines on Milton, his blindness and his writing of *Paradise Lost*. It was published along with other poems by his son John Hampden-Trevor, who was plenipotentiary at Turin from 15 October 1783 through 1798, in Parma in 1792 (see 92–93): *Britannia, Lathmon, Villa Romhamensis* (Parmæ In Edibvs Palatinis Typis Bodonianis cl 1 cc xcii).

17. Excerpts from Parsons's "Epistle from Naples":

Nurs'd in the navel of thy native land,
To thee it's Genius with unsparing hand
Dealt the rich products of that happy clime,
The Patriot's flame, the Poet's flight sublime,
Strong sense, unsullied honor, faithful love!
Then led thy step thro' foreign plains to rove
That neighboring nations might admiring see
What genuine Britons are, or ought to be.
    Me Nature form'd with less exalted views,
An humble friend of Virtue and the Muse,
Yet early bade my panting soul aspire
Above the sordid wish, the low desire,
Scorn groveling Vice, and pity Folly's brood,
The wise to honour, and revere the good, . . .
If Baia's shores invite my wondering eye
Those humbled haunts of pride and luxury,
Pensive I view, with retrospective thought,
What changes there the wizard Time hath wrought,
Through mouldering walls sulphureous vapors rise,
The once-gay bath a shapeless ruin lies,
Low in the wave the crumbling villa falls,
And boats ride tilting o'er the marble halls!
    . . . O Greatheed! haste, the tedious rains are o'er,
And Spring diffusive spreads her bloomy store;
Here joys excursive through an ampler field
Shall charm thee more than all e'en Rome can yield,
Tho' that great seat of empire and of art
Of ancient pride preserve a larger part; . . .
Fire in 'mid ocean throws a new-born isle,
Where flame once raged the wat'ry mirrors smile;

Where once the eye no verdure could explore,
In glades and glooms behold the tusked boar!
Where barren tracts the late eruption shew,
Waste is the scene—to fertilize anew,
Plains rise to mountains, mountains sink to plains,
Yet o'er the dread confusion ORDER reigns!

Excerpts from Parsons's "Vallombrosa":

Sov'reign of th'enraptur'd soul,
That willing owns thy mild controul,
Contemplation, hither come!
I have lov'd with thee to roam
Wild Helvetia's steeps between,
And gaze upon each wond'rous scene;
Whether, when the morning light
Gilds the Glacier's lofty height,
Where the broken fragments lie,
Fancy bade my wand'ring eye
In the icy mass admire
Many an arc, and many a spire,
Like the labor'd works of stone,
By the hand of Time o'erthrown.
Or, when Phoebus o'er my head
His strait-down rays at noon had shed, . . .
    Florence now I leave behind,
Thro' the length'ning valley wind,
There but fruitless is my toil,
Little yields th'ungrateful soil,
Save the clust'ring grapes that shine
Depending from th'empurpled vine.
Now the mountain's foot I gain,
And to the Convent rise with pain;
Vallombrosa, sacred shade!
For Peace and meek Devotion made;
Safe from pangs the worldling knows,
Here secure in calm repose,
Far from life's perplexing maze,
The pious Fathers pass their days; . . .
    But chief my raptur'd gaze I throw
On th'extended view below;
Arno, many a Poet's theme,
Now appears a trifling stream,

While my curious sight I strain
To find its distant source in vain, . . .
The Muse on my lone path shall shine,
And Contemplation's wealth be mine!

NOTES TO CHAPTER NINE

1. *The Prose Works of John Milton, with a Biographical Introduction*, ed. R.W. Griswold (Philadelphia: Hooker, 1845), I, 1.
2. See my essays "The Poet in the Poem: John Milton's Presence in *Paradise Lost*," *The CEA Critic* 48/49 (Summer/Fall 1986): 32–55, for Eliot and Zukofsky; "Influence for the Worse?: Hart Crane Rethinks Milton," *The Visionary Company* 1–2 (1983): 71–89; "*Paradise Lost*: 'Erased,' " *Milton Quarterly* 16 (1982): 80–81.

NOTES TO CHAPTER TEN

1. For one instance, see my essay, " 'They that dwell under his shadow shall return': Joyce's *Chamber Music* and Milton," 200–09 in *New Alliances in Joyce Studies: 'When it's Aped to Foul a Delfian'*, ed. Bonnie Kime Scott (Newark: University of Delaware Press, 1988).
2. "Kafka y sus precursores", *La Nación* 19 (August 1951); *Borges A Reader A Selection from the Writings of Jorge Luis Borges*, ed. Emir Rodriguez Monegal and Alastair Reid (New York: E. P. Dutton, 1981), 243.
3. *With Mortal Voice: The Creation of Paradise Lost* (Lexington: University Press of Kentucky, 1982), 137.

Index

(Generally Shakespeare's specific works and analogues from other authors, as well as critics, cited in chapter one, are omitted from this index.)

181

Index

Index

Index

Index

Voltaire, 113, 119, 122–23, 126, 130, 170 n. 7

Walker, John, 46
Walker, Joseph Cooper, 123–24
Walker, Mary (Lady Hamilton), 90–92, 101, 104–106
Waller, Edmund, 76
Walsh, I., 125
Warburton, William, 6
Warton, Joseph, 43, 82
Warton, Thomas, 41, 43–44, 47–48
Webb, Daniel, 52
Wesley, John, 51
Wesley, Samuel, 170 n. 5
West, Jane, 94
Whalley, Peter, 51
White, Robert, 45
Whitley, Alvin, 172 n. 14
Whitman, Walt, 154
Wilde, Oscar, 158

Wilkins, John, 6
Williams, Peter, 46
Wittreich, Joseph A., 90
Wollaston, William, 170 n. 5
Wollstonecraft, Mary, 95, 101, 108–10, 173 second n. 2
Woodhouse, A. S. P., and Bush, Douglas, 2
Wordsworth, Christopher, 142
Wordsworth, William, 4, 56, 66–67, 76, 82–84, 86, 133, 137

Yalden, Thomas, 141
Yearsley, Ann, 47, 84
Yeats, William Butler, 4, 158–59, 163, 172 n. 15
Young, Edward, 43, 109
Young Senator, The, 51

Zanotti, Francesco Maria, 129
Zukofsky, Louis, 152

187

About the Author

JOHN T. SHAWCROSS is professor of English at the University of Kentucky. He is also the author of *Paradise Regain'd: Worthy T'Have Not Remain'd So Long Unsung* (Duquesne University Press, 1988), *With Mortal Voice: The Creation of Paradise Lost* (University Press of Kentucky, 1982) and *Milton: A Bibliography for the Years 1624–1700* (Medieval & Renaissance Texts & Studies), which won the James Holly Hanford Award of the Milton Society of America as the most distinguished book on Milton published in 1984.